The Language of the Soul

Healing with Words of Truth

By John L. Payne

© John L. Payne 2006

The right of John L. Payne to be identified as the author of this work has been asserted by him in accordance with the Copyright, Designs and Patents Act 1998.

First published in English by Findhorn Press 2006

ISBN 10: 1-84409-076-0
ISBN 13: 978-1-84409-076-1

All rights reserved. The contents of this book may not be reproduced in any form, except for short extracts for quotation or review, without the written permission of the publisher.

British Library Cataloguing-in-Publication Data.
A catalogue record for this book is available from the British Library.

Edited by Kristen Bottger and Jean Semrau
Cover design by Damian Keenan
Interior design by Pam Bochel
Printed and bound by WS Bookwell, Finland

Published by
Findhorn Press
305A The Park,
Findhorn, Forres
Scotland IV36 3TE

Tel 01309 690582
Fax 01309 690036
email: info@findhornpress.com

www.findhornpress.com

The Language of the Soul

TABLE OF CONTENTS

Prologue – The Path of Healing	i
Acknowledgments	v
Introduction	vii
What is a Family Constellation?	1
Chapter One: The Stories We Tell	3
Chapter Two: Expressing the Language of the Soul	21
Chapter Three: Retrieving the Lost Soul	59
Chapter Four: To Whom Do I Belong? – Adoptees	89
Chapter Five: Addictions and Substance Abuse: Relieving a Hole in the Soul	107
Chapter Six: Whose Life Is It, Anyway?	135
Chapter Seven: Ancestral Inheritance	147
Chapter Eight: Making Clear Apologies	153
Epilogue	161
Further Information and Contacts	165

PROLOGUE

THE PATH OF HEALING

Many times on my own journey towards healing, I have come to the crossroads where I've needed to make the choice between having peace and being right about something. Very often we try to make ourselves bigger by holding on to our opinion about what is right above all else, even when it clearly does not serve us to do so. For many of us, being "right" has become equal to survival. We feel that if we are in some way "wrong", that would mean our certain demise.

On the path of personal healing, we need to develop the skill of objectivity, which is quite an achievement in itself as so many of us have so much invested in our stories. Our stories often keep us exactly where we are, and, for the most part, they feel very safe to us. When we stay exactly where we are, we need not change, we need not take responsibility for our current life circumstances. We can simply stick to our story and feel very "right" about it. The path of healing requires a willingness to be totally honest. I don't mean in the way that most of us interpret honesty as being able to express an opinion liberally, but honesty in terms of being able to acknowledge clearly what is. In addition, we need to know the boundary between that which is our own business and that which belongs to another. At times we find justification in being involved in other people's business, especially when it comes to our parents. We say things like, "But I'm affected by their unhappy marriage". Here we have that magic word "but", and in observation of myself and others, everything that is said after the "but" is usually just a story, none of our business, an excuse, or simply not true.

Courage. The path of healing not only requires a willingness to be honest and to acknowledge what is; it takes courage. It takes courage to face our errors of judgment, our arrogance, our stubbornness, our rage and even our pain. We grow up in a world where we are encouraged not to be honest, whilst at the same time we are clearly told that to lie is a sin. Perhaps you remember a time when you heard a parent complain about Aunt Sally, stating just how much they don't like her, then miraculously Aunt Sally either arrives or calls on the phone, and you witness affection and kind words being showered upon her. Or perhaps you observed one parent telling the other, "Tell them I'm out". These are very mixed and confusing messages that are sent to us as children, and we soon learnt that not only was telling a lie a sin, but being honest about our feelings was also a grave sin. Many of us feel deeply ashamed about the deeper feelings that we carry, perhaps feeling that we are in some way weak, or a failure, and therefore to expose those deeper feelings means to risk losing face.

So many of us have had the experience of being able to run in circles around counselors and psychotherapists as we feign triumph in having been able to solve one or another issue. We are intelligent, quick-witted, and we are able to work out precisely what needs to be said, make all the right noises, just to avoid "that" subject ever coming up again for us to deal with. When it doesn't quite work for us, then we can easily move on to either another therapist, yet another "empowerment" workshop, or skip to a different modality altogether. Why do we do this? Even though our lives may not be working in the way we ideally want them to work, we have become accustomed to them and the discomfort falls within our comfort zone, so to speak. It is almost like sitting in an uncomfortable chair; the longer we sit in it, the more comfortable it actually becomes.

Over the past year of working intensely, I have been deeply humbled by the courage I have witnessed with many of my clients. One client, I shall call her Janet, wished to work on the subject of an abortion, a subject that frequently arises in Family Constellation work as it very often has an impact on a family system. As she revealed her story, I began to realize that this was no ordinary story of abortion. She had had an abortion in the fourth month of pregnancy and had seen her daughter move arms and legs in a kidney dish immediately afterwards. I was faced with the question, "Is this abortion or is this murder?" and "When does abortion become a murder?" I decided in that moment that to ponder even this question was really none of my business so I approached this case from the perspective of decisions that either serve our greater good or do not. This client was able to risk judgment, face her own remorse, guilt, shame and grief and come to a place of accepting the consequences of her actions with great dignity. This is a rare gift to witness and to be a part of; I bow to her. Another client, I shall call her Josephine, faced her greatest fear of admitting that she had knowingly allowed her husband and his friend to sexually abuse her daughter.

Prologue – The Path of Healing

Working in the setting of Family Constellations, we become quickly accustomed to the fact that little, or nothing, is hidden. The *language of the Soul* facilitates this. When truth is spoken, and we hear it, we relax; when truth is expressed through us, we relax. The truth actually feels good, even when it is a hurdle to get there. The language of the Soul is poetic and resonates with the love of the Soul. When we have touched and experienced this many times, clients like Janet and Josephine find the courage to face their most horrific stories as they know through experience, and also instinctively, that there is safety in the Soul.

Arrogance. Our own arrogance is one of the greatest demons that we need to face. One client of mine, when facing her "fate" in a constellation (I will define this later) became acutely aware of her own arrogance of "knowing better" and wanting to challenge it comically said, "I feel like a Chihuahua barking at a Doberman, it's ridiculous!". Often, as a defence mechanism, we simply try to convince ourselves that we are bigger (Doberman), more important, know what is right, and forget that when it comes to the question of fate we are merely Chihuahuas and the best thing we can do is simply accept what is. We must also be willing to release all of our stories, hidden loyalties and opinions.

Humility. At times we can get tied up in the idea that our intellectual understanding of our own and our families' issues in some way make us special or more important. Perhaps we even wear our wounds like medals from the battlefield and clutch at them for dear life in the fear that someone may have the audacity to remove our longstanding identity. In my observation, when we are stuck in martyrdom, arrogance is always hot on our heels. When we get to the stage of knowing that we are just ordinary people with ordinary problems, we will tackle them in an ordinary and honest way. That doesn't mean that we either minimalise or deny our problems, but it does mean not building them up so that we can compare wounds with another in a "mine is bigger than yours" mentality. Part of the path of humility understands the power of fate and that there are certain things that we cannot change. We can't change our parents, we cannot change the fact that our ancestors died in a war or in the Holocaust. However, we can change how we feel about it, and leave fate's business to fate. When the Chihuahua barks itself silly at the Doberman, it exhausts itself in the process, perhaps even going hoarse and what does the Doberman do? It simply stares back, knowing that it is far bigger and that the Chihuahua will have no impact. We may very well protest and say, "But the thing that happened was so wrong", to which our Soul will reply, "But it's a done deal, it can't be changed".

What we can change are our belief systems and our feelings on certain subjects. There is much grace and peace in that path.

With love,
John Payne
(Chihuahua still learning not to bother barking at the Doberman)

ACKNOWLEDGMENTS

My gratitude goes to Thierry Bogliolo my publisher at Findhorn Press for continuing to support my work and my writing, for his patience, encouragement and presence.

Firstly I would like to acknowledge my students and regular clients that have contributed so much to my growth with this work: Sam Weber, Gail Wrogemann, Paula Damaskinos, Helga Fuehrer, Christiane Schulze-Kirschner, Robert Howes, Mirna Palma, Jonathan Atkins, Rashnee Parhanse-Atkins, Tania Wroe, Jayne Davies, Sue Tomkinson, Margaret Rawicz, Sascha Ernst, Diane Du Preez, Patricia Gradidge, Kay Roos, Sue Head, Allyson Logan, Philip Johnson plus many, many more. Each of them bringing their own story and their own unique ability to heal through dauntless honesty and unwavering courage. You are my inspiration!

In addition, I would like to thank those people in the media that have given me many opportunities to share my work and my vision with countless viewers, readers and listeners: Presenter Noelene Maholwana-Sanqu and producer Msizi Nkosi from SABC3's 3Talk show, Kate Turkington, Leigh Bennie, Katie McNally and Dr D from Radio 702, Carol Ann Jamieson from Odyssey Magazine, Kathy Hearn from SABC3's 'Free Spirit' team, Yoga Teachers Fellowship of Southern Africa and Complete Yoga Magazine, Mariette Snyman of 'Rooi Rose' magazine, Caroline Chapman of Renaissance Magazine plus many others.

A special thank you to Albrecht Mahr, Bertold Ulsamer, Iyanla Vanzant , Jamie Faust and Drindy Keller for writing encouraging endorsements of my first book on this subject.

A very special mention must go to Carol Kulig. A dear friend, enormously talented healer, confidante and advisor. My world and my work have been immeasurably blessed by your presence in my life. Also a thank you to Joan Osterloh for introducing me to the powerful work of the Clairvision School.

Thank you to my dearest friends for loving me and respecting me as I am and for encouraging my work with your love and support: Annebiene Pilon, Gerrit Koelers, Paulo Monica and Hilda de la Rosa.

Great thanks go to my housekeeper Rosinha, without whom I would simply not have the time to write books. Thank you for your laughter, your smiles, and for anticipating my needs. Obrigado!

Last, but not least. I must acknowledge and thank my stepmother, Lee Butler-Payne. You stepped into my life just a short while after the death of my mother, and did so with great grace, love and respect. I am deeply grateful to you. Thank you for all the times you were my biggest fan and called me enthusiastically after every TV and Radio appearance. You have made a great difference in my life. I love you.

John Payne
Johannesburg, South Africa
2006

INTRODUCTION

Truth is a very rare commodity, even amongst friends and family. Is it that we lie to one another? Sometimes we do. Or is it more that we really don't have a good understanding of what truth is? Perceptions of truth differ greatly from one person to another, and one of the biggest traps we all fall into is not knowing the difference between speaking our truth and expressing an opinion. So how can we know when we are speaking the truth? Through the pages of this book, I will seek to demonstrate to you through example how truth has a specific feeling and that when we speak the truth, we feel a deep sense of relief as we express the language of the Soul in uncomplicated ways.

Much of my observation of truth being spoken comes from my many years of experience working with *Family Constellations*, a profound healing modality originally developed by Bert Hellinger. In my first book on this topic, *The Healing of Individuals, Families and Nations*, I introduced the power of *healing sentences* as used in a Family Constellations context. Now I would like to offer you a way of taking the principles of healing sentences that can be used in day-to-day life, allowing you to speak the *language of the Soul* in ways that are liberating for you and also for those around you – friends, lovers, spouses, loved ones, your family and colleagues. Through the pages of this book, I will present case study Family Constellations where the therapeutic power of distilled healing sentences will come to life.

Our definition of what is truth, or what is true, shifts like sands in the desert. Each day new ripples of truth appear and sometimes personal truths can grow into large sand dunes. Dunes, however, can change shape, move, or disappear overnight, literally blown away by the winds of change. What is always true about a dune is that it is made up of grains of sand. Simple truth is that a grain of sand; it is what is left over once the structures that we have built around our truths begin to dissolve.

With the process of Family Constellations, we look at simple truths; we examine the grain of sand, so to speak. The simplest truth for all human beings is the truth of love. All of us seek to love and our loyalty to those we love knows no bounds. One example of this was a client making an inner movement towards accepting her alcoholic father. There were a number of simple truths. First, "My father is an alcoholic and there is nothing I can do to change it", second, "Much of my life has been spent resisting this truth, wanting to change fate". The third truth is "This is my father, the one and only, I have no other", and the fourth truth, the one that can be accessed when we release resistance is, "I love my father deeply". When we get down to this one grain of sand, we begin to see that the energy we have expended in building a sand dune has been at a very high cost, for all we needed all along was this one grain of sand, the simple truth: I love my father. When we submit unconditionally to love, we are liberated beyond all that which we have known. Simple truths belong to the realm of the Soul and the rewards are immeasurable.

Most of us live our lives through our own perception of truth, much of it being either an illusion or a straightforward lie. So how do we develop these multiple versions of truth and, more importantly, how do these versions of truth or stories we have told ourselves sabotage our lives?

Within the pages of this book, I will share with you my knowledge and experiences, both personal and professional, gained through working with many hundreds of individuals over the past decade, most of it within the context of Family Constellation work. I seek to take you on a journey where you will not only intellectually understand the *language of the Soul*, but also begin to feel its unwavering truth resonate throughout your entire being and touch your heart in some way.

On working with Family Constellations, healing sentences have become an integral part of the process, bringing unbridled truth to any given situation. As healing sentences are simple truths, devoid of masks and pretences, they form a way in which we can all communicate on a day-to-day basis within our relationships, friendships and families. When truth is made simple, pain, disputes and illusions can be dispelled more easily.

This book will seek to answer the following questions:

> Why do we lie?
>
> How do we know when we are telling the absolute truth?
>
> How do we create truth within a relationship?
>
> How are wounds healed with simple truths?
>
> How are we supposed to apologise?
>
> When is it appropriate to withhold the truth?

Introduction

This book will take you through a step-by-step process of knowing what truth is and the difference between speaking your truth and expressing an opinion. It will give you many examples that you can easily apply to your own life. In addition, examples of Family Constellation processes will be given, in order to demonstrate the healing power of truth when it is spoken and assist you in seeing the greater truth of your own relationships as the stories unfold. When we speak truth, we touch love. Truth accepts what is, and love is the acceptance of what is.

WHAT IS A FAMILY CONSTELLATION?

In my first book on this topic, The Healing of Individuals, Families and Nations, the first two chapters are dedicated to giving a detailed explanation of Family Constellations as a modality, the use of the knowing field, representation, systemic entanglements, healing sentences, causes and solutions. Following is a very brief summary, along with an explanation of some of the terminology used in that book.

What is a Family Constellation and how is it set up?

When an individual wishes to work on a relationship issue, a theme in their life or an illness, we seek to look at entanglements within a family system that may be at the root of disruptive life patterns.

Family Constellations is event-oriented inasmuch as we take little to no account of personality descriptions or any particular bias or "story" that a client may have. In setting up a constellation, we are specifically interested in *who* is a member of the family system and *what* specifically happened.

Events of significance that often have impact on a family system include:
- The early death of parents or grandparents
- Miscarriages, stillbirths and abortions
- Murders, tragic and accidental deaths
- Sudden loss of partner/spouse
- Adoptions
- Broken engagements and divorce
- War experiences
- Victims and perpetrators of crime and injustice
- Family secrets
- Individuals who have been forced out of a family or disowned.

During a brief pre-constellation interview, the client is asked about who is in the family and if there have been any specific events that have occurred in the family, such as those listed above. Once the information is gathered, the client is then asked to select participants in the workshop to represent members of their family and any significant individuals, be they grandparents, uncles, aunts, etc., whose lives may have been impacted by events typical of the list above. Once all of the representatives have been chosen, they are placed intuitively in a standing pattern on the workshop floor space and it is at this point that the constellation comes to life.

The knowing field

The great difference between Family Constellation work and psychodrama or "role play" is that the representatives are not acting out roles according to personality descriptions given by the client or responding to the client's "story" about what went on in the family.

With the set-up of a constellation, the representatives move into and become part of *the knowing field* of the family and remarkably take on the actual feelings and impulses of the real family members. This process is a deep experience not only for the representatives, but also for the client as they watch their family come to life in front of them. (The term, *knowing field,* was initially coined by Dr. Albrecht Mahr in 1997 at the first international conference on Family Constellations in Wiesloch, near Heidelberg, Germany.)

The process

Once a Family Constellation is set up, the facilitator first observes the set-up in silence, observing both the body language and the pattern that has been created. Very often, the facilitator is able to see indications of certain events that have taken place within the family simply from observing how the representatives are standing in relationship to one another and their overall demeanour, even when the client has made no mention of specific events.

Once these preliminary observations have been made, the facilitator then walks to each representative and asks them how they are feeling. The feelings reported can be physical descriptions or a wide variety of emotional states.

When problems and entanglements are identified, I as the facilitator then use healing sentences to bring about resolution. (An entanglement is identified when an individual is "tied up" in the fate or business of another. Very often, hidden loyalties are revealed to the extent that a client can be literally carrying and living out both the feelings and the fate of another from their extended family system.) The healing sentences are the "language of the Soul," about which this book is written.

Chapter One
THE STORIES WE TELL

We have all learnt from an early age that to lie is unacceptable; however, we all seem to do it with great regularity, if not on a daily basis, not least to ourselves. We also understand that to be caught out lying means the risk of punishment when we are children, and the withdrawal of friendship and love when we are adults. As children, we learn at a very young age that being "bad" means that love will be withdrawn and that being "good" means that we will be showered with approval and affection. As children, we all understand that we are totally dependent upon our parents for sustenance and that without their care and love, we would simply die. Therefore, it is imperative in the child's mind to preserve the love and approval of parents; it is a natural survival instinct. All this translates into a model that we use as adults for communicating with one another, and this model creates stories that take us away from distilled truth to a version that very often perpetuates our own wounds and the wounds that we have inflicted upon others, unwittingly or otherwise.

So it would seem that all of the lies and stories that we tell and live are motivated from a place of wanting to preserve love, which in turn assures our survival. For what can live without love? However, the lies we end up living and telling ourselves and those around us can at times also serve as a way to avoid responsibility for what is. Within Family Constellation work we see the more complex issues of *hidden loyalties* within the family system, which can cause us to hold onto a story that simply isn't true, or one that has little foundation in reality. Let us take a look.

Connie
"I seem to have problems with my relationships with men"

Payne to Connie: Have you ever been married or had a long-term relationship with a man? An engagement or similar?

Connie: No. All of my relationships have been short lived.

Payne: Any miscarriages or abortions?

Connie: No, nothing like that.

Payne: So please tell me about your family in terms of who is in your family and any special events that took place in terms of early deaths, tragedies etc.

Connie: Well, my father was a very bad father, he was a womaniser

Payne: That's an interesting response to my question, because it is not the one that I asked for, but a revealing response nonetheless.

Connie: Well, in my mind he wasn't a good father and my mother suffered because of it.

Payne: Are they still married?

Connie: Yes, but they shouldn't be.

Payne: Goodness, you are quite entangled in your parents' affairs. I often see this with individuals who report having difficulty in forming stable relationships; they are far too tied up with something else.

Connie's "truth" is that her father is a "very bad father". This in itself creates a prison in terms of her relationship with men in general, as she has little respect for the primary man in her life. Let us now look at what her Family Constellation reveals.

Payne to Connie: Please remember, Connie, that although we look at truths in a very direct, perhaps exposing way, there is no judgment about your belief that your father was a bad father. There is usually a more complex hidden issue behind your belief, perhaps one that you yourself do not know of, or simply cannot see. One thing I would say to you is that, irrespective of your feelings, your mother has *chosen* to stay with your father. Would you say that that was *your* business or *her* business?

Connie: Well, it is her business, but…. *(Payne laughs)*

Payne: There always seems to be a "but" with these stories.

Connie: *(Laughing as well)* I see your point.

Payne: Well, let us set up your constellation because we don't want to get bogged down in defending positions. It's far better to allow the constellation to reveal what is. Are you ready to work?

Connie: Yes, that's a good idea, what do I need to do?

Payne: Just look around the room and select individuals to represent your father, mother, yourself, your brother and your sister.

Chapter One – The Stories We Tell

Connie looks around the room and selects individuals to represent herself, her mother, her father, her brother and her sister. She then places them in a standing pattern on the workshop floor. The pattern that the family stands in reveals much in terms of the relationships within the family and often indicates events that have taken place, even when the client has not spoken of such things.

Connie's constellation

C: Connie   F: Father   M: Mother   S: Son   D2: Daughter 2
MB: miscarried brother

Figure 1

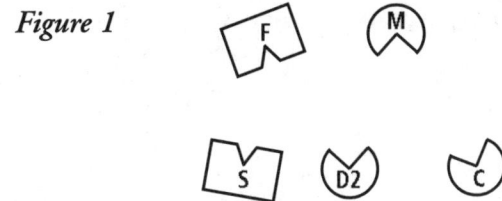

Payne to Connie: When I look at this set-up, a few things come to mind. Firstly, you look as if you are on the outside looking in.

Connie: Yes, that's how I feel.

Payne: Also, your father looks very sad. But let's look a little more closely.

Payne walks to representatives and begins to enquire about their feelings.

Payne to Father: How are things here?

Father: I feel sad, I can't really look up. If I do, I want to look down again.

Payne to Mother: How are things here?

Mother: I don't really want to look at my husband and it is difficult to look at my children. I feel very sad when I see my husband out of the corner of my eye.

Payne to Son: How are you?

Son: I want to be close to my father, I'm aware of my two sisters and mother, but my feeling is to be closer to my father.

Payne to Connie: Both of your parents seem very sad. What else happened in the family?

Connie: As I said, my father had many affairs.

Payne: What we are witnessing here has nothing to do with affairs. Affairs are symptoms of something else, and what we are seeing is that "something else" and we need to work with that. Were there any other pregnancies?

Connie: Yes, my parents were very young, I think in their late teens, and my mother got pregnant and lost the child. It was a miscarriage, not a stillbirth; my mother mentioned it once many years ago.

Payne takes a representative from the workshop audience and places her in front of the parents to stand in for the miscarried child.

Figure 2

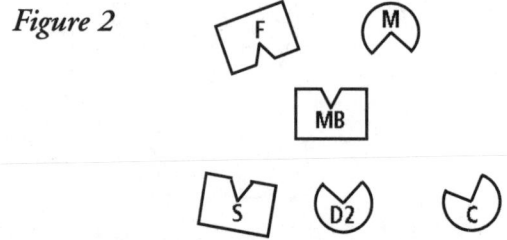

Payne to Father and Mother: How is that when I place this miscarried child in front of you both?

Mother: Unbearable, it feels like a terrible loss.

Father: My heart is very heavy.

Payne to Miscarriage: How are things with you?

Miscarried child: I'm a boy!

Payne notices that Connie is sobbing in her chair as she watches the constellation unfold.

Payne to Connie: How are you doing?

Connie: When she said, "I'm a boy", I suddenly remembered that I used to have a childhood fantasy about having another brother somewhere. I dismissed it as I grew older. This all makes so much sense to me now. It hurts me to see my father so sad.

Payne asks the miscarried brother to place his head on the shoulders of his parents as they stand together. It is a very moving scene as they can feel their loss during a teenage pregnancy. After a few moments the constellation proceeds with healing sentences.

Payne to Parents: Please look directly at your child, into his eyes, and say, "Beloved child, it is a pity that you could not stay, for we have missed you greatly".

Chapter One – The Stories We Tell

Both representatives for the parents repeat the healing sentence.

Payne to Father & Mother: Now say to your child, "We now give you a place in our hearts and a place in the family as our first child".

As the representatives for Connie's parents say these words, not only do her parents breathe a sigh of relief, but so do Connie and the representatives for her brother and sister. When the language of the Soul is spoken, it gives relief and we witness that with an outward sigh that relaxes the body.

Payne now rearranges the constellation, placing each member in their proper place.

Figure 3

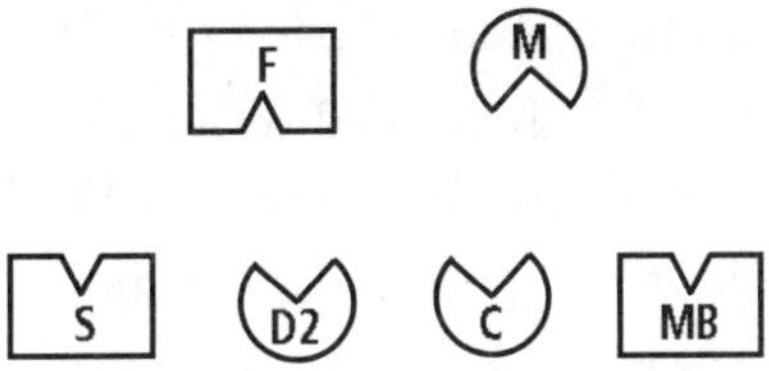

Payne to Parents: Please say to one another in turn, "The loss was too much to bear, so I turned away from you".

Father to Mother: "The loss was too great to bear, so I turned away from you". *As the representative says these words, he breaks down in tears and embraces his wife and says, "I've missed her so much".*

Payne to Connie: How does it feel when you see this?

Connie: It's very sad. I feel my heart opening towards my father, I feel very sad for him and sad that I withdrew from him out of loyalty to my mother.

Payne to Mother: Please look at your daughter Connie and say, "Whatever happened between your father and me, leave it with us. I chose to stay with him and chose him to be your father".

Mother to Connie: "Whatever happened between your father and me, leave it with us. I chose to stay with him and chose him to be your father".

Payne to Mother: How does it feel when you say that?

Mother: It's a relief, and it's true.

Payne to Connie: How does this new picture feel?

Connie: Strangely enough, although I've never given this miscarriage any thought, it just makes sense to me, and like everyone else, I feel relieved. It also feels like I have less pressure on me because I am not the firstborn any longer.

Payne to Connie: And what do you feel that you have learnt from this constellation?

Connie: To mind my own business? *(Payne and workshop attendees laugh.)*

Payne: Indeed. Perhaps the most important insight is that it is your mother's choice to remain with your father and that you as a daughter are obliged to respect that as it is truly none of your business. None of us can ever truly know what happens in a relationship; we can only ever observe it from the outside and interpret it through our own perceptions. Truth is often something quite different. And your story about your father being a "bad father"?

Connie: This has definitely shed some new light on the subject and I feel much softer towards him. However, I've had this view of him for so long, I think it will possibly take time for it to totally transform.

Payne: All you need to remember is that your mother has chosen to stay, and to respect her decision in that. It is never wise for children to become entangled in their parents' affairs.

Conclusion

Connie, like many of us, has been living with a story that has little or no foundation in fact. Her story was "my father is a bad father", but what is revealed when we shine the light of inescapable truth onto this story? We see a man who deeply cares for his wife and who felt devastated at the loss of his child, a wife who turned away from him when the grief became too much, and a choice that Connie's mother has made that is none of Connie's business. In essence, what would have been the more truthful statement: "My father was a bad father" or "I don't respect my mother's choices"?

In order to free ourselves of unnecessary burdens, we first need to examine if we are entangled in something that has nothing to do with us in the first place.

Healing sentences in Family Constellation work are the language of the Soul. When we use such distilled truths, we become liberated from entanglements and once we witness the power of this way of working, we can begin to integrate this liberating way of communicating in our day-to-day lives.

Let us look at examples of communication based on "story", compared to using the *language of the Soul*. I will use Connie's story. Let us imagine that

Chapter One – The Stories We Tell

Connie now wants to apologise to her mother for her attitude and conduct within the family. I would encourage you to sit back and try to feel in your body how you respond to each sentence and ask yourself which example is truer for you in day-to-day life.

Connie 1: "Mum, I'm really sorry for my bad attitude towards Dad and the tensions it has caused in the family. I've found his womanizing to be a problem for me and I really don't like it. But, you know, he is your husband, so I respect your decision to stay with him".

Connie 2: "Mum, I'm deeply sorry for disrespecting your decisions. It's between you and Dad and it is none of my business".

Which of the two sentences do you think would have brought relief not only to Connie, but also to her mother? The second example shows how the *language of the Soul* does not hide behind masks; it is clear and to the point. Having said that, it is neither blunt nor brutal, but simply crystal clear. We can tell when truth is spoken by how our body feels when we speak it. Usually there will be an outward sigh of relief, perhaps coupled with the relaxation of the shoulders. Untruths are retained in the body, and truth flows freely.

Why then do we make apologising so difficult and fill our sentences with stories? Mostly it is because we believe that if we give more reasons to explain our behaviour, the other party will be more forgiving and, more importantly, the love will be preserved. However, in truth, the longer the story, the less likely that our transgression will be accepted and forgiven by the other.

Let us look at another example.

Richard

"My wife is so cold towards me"

Payne to Richard: What would you like to work with today?

Richard: My marriage. My wife is very cold towards me. We are rarely intimate and she is not the least bit affectionate, almost from the time we first got married some five years ago.

Payne: Have there been any significant events during the marriage such as miscarriages or stillbirths?

Richard: No.

Payne: Have either of you been married, engaged or otherwise seriously involved before?

The Language of the Soul

Richard: No. We were in our early twenties when we met, and apart from dating a few people, there was nothing particularly serious for either of us.

Payne also enquires about any significant events within Richard's and his wife's families of origin.

Payne: OK, I have sufficient information for now. Let's keep it simple. Take representatives for yourself and your wife and we'll see what happens.

Richard chooses a man to represent himself and a woman to represent his wife and places them in a standing position on the workshop floor according to his feeling.

R: Richard   W: Wife   CS: Childhood Sweetheart

Figure 1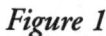

Payne to Richard: I notice that you have placed them very far apart.

Richard: Well, that is how it feels.

Payne: Let's take a closer look.

Payne steps into the "field" of the constellation and approaches Richard's representative.

Payne to Richard's Representative: I notice that you are leaning quite far to the right. What's happening?

Richard's Representative: It feels like a magnetic pull, I can't help it. I actually want to turn and look in the direction to which I am leaning.

Payne: OK, follow your impulse.

Richard's representative turns and faces the direction in which he was leaning.

Figure 2

Chapter One – The Stories We Tell

Payne to Richard's Representative: How is that now?

Richard's Representative: I feel transfixed and very, very sad.

Payne to Wife's representative: And how is this for you?

Wife: I really don't want him to look there. I feel a little angry and I have a slight knot in my stomach.

Payne to Richard the client: Was there anyone who "stood beside you" who perhaps died or left in some way?

Richard: Not that I can think of.

Payne: Are you sure? The constellation is indicating that someone "stood beside you" who was important to you and is no longer here.

Richard sheds a tear and now has difficulty talking.

Richard: Now I remember, but it was so long ago. When I was fifteen years old, I had my very first girlfriend at school. She was my first kiss. She took an overdose and died.

Payne takes a woman from the workshop and places her in front of Richard's representative in order to represent Richard's childhood sweetheart.

Figure 3

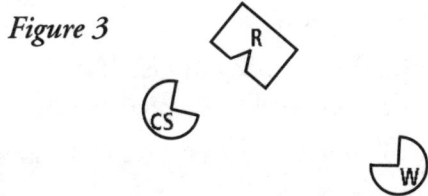

Both Richard and his representative break down in tears. Richard's representative flings his arms around the woman in front of him and sobs loudly on her shoulders and utters, "I couldn't save you, I couldn't save you".

Payne moves across to Richard and sits next to him, placing a hand gently on his shoulders.

Payne to Richard: This is a deeply held grief. It also seems that you feel guilty for her death in some way.

Richard: Yes, that's true. I've tried my best to forget this and now I see it in front of me like this. It is like it never went away.

Payne: We tend to bury deep pain like this. So much so, that when I asked you about previous significant relationships or events, you could not recall this. But let us work further.

Payne to Wife's Representative: How is it for you when you see this?

Wife's Representative: I have very mixed feelings. I cried with him when I saw this and a part of me is very sad. However, another part of me feels very jealous and quite angry with him. I want him to be looking at me and not at her.

Payne asks Richard's representative to sit down and he takes Richard in his place to stand in front of his childhood sweetheart.

Payne to Richard: What was her name?

Richard: Joanne.

Payne to Richard: Please say to Joanne, "I couldn't save you".

Richards says the sentence to Joanne, barely being able to get his words out through the grief.

Payne to Richard: Now say to her, "There was nothing I could do to save you".

Richard says the sentence to Joanne and sighs as he does so.

Payne to Richard: How does that feel now?

Richard: Much better. It's true, I couldn't do anything at all, but I still felt guilty. I feel clearer on this now.

Payne: We are not quite finished. Say to her, "Dear Joanne, you were my first love and I loved you dearly, as a boy would".

Richard: Dear Joanne, you were my first love and I loved you dearly as a boy would.

Payne: How does that feel?

Richard: Saying, "as a boy would", made a big difference; it has placed it in the past, in my childhood, even though I was fifteen. I can now see myself as a man who has a wife.

Payne: *(Smiling)* Perhaps your wife can love you now that you are a man? Let us see.

Payne turns Richard around to look at his wife across the room, then slowly moves his wife to a position standing to his left next to him.

Payne to Wife: How does that feel to be next to him?

Wife: I can look at him now and I want to get closer.

Payne to Richard: Say to your wife, "I'm sorry, I was looking at Joanne and couldn't see you".

Richard: I'm sorry, I was looking at Joanne and I couldn't see you.

Payne: How does that feel, Richard?

Richard: It feels like there is hope for us now, like I can release Joanne and really turn towards my wife. I had no idea that I was part of the problem, but I can't deny this now. It feels good, really good to have worked with this.

Conclusion

The healing sentence, "I'm sorry, I was looking at Joanne and I couldn't see you", created unambiguous resolution for Richard, enabling him to plainly see that it was not just his wife who had turned away from him, but that he had never really looked at her. When we distil truth in this way, giving it clear and unmistakable language, it not only brings relief, but also provides us with the tools to heal our relationships. Let us now imagine that Richard returns home to his wife and attempts to explain what has been going on.

Richard 1: "My therapist has allowed me to see that I'm still hung up on my childhood sweetheart who committed suicide. It's been really difficult for me to let that go and I've been feeling very resentful because you have gone so cold towards me".

Richard 2: "Today I've realized that I've been looking at Joanne all this time. I'm sorry for that".

Which explanation feels better? Perhaps imagine that you are the wife hearing your husband say this. How does it feel? The clearer and simpler we are in what we say to others, the greater the opportunity for healing.

In summary, we must ask the question: was Richard's story really true? Did his wife turn away from him? What the work revealed was that Richard appeared to be only looking at Joanne, his childhood sweetheart, and so it would seem that his wife turned away from him as a result of that. What wife could measure up to a childhood sweetheart who was now with the dead? Such loves are held in an idealistic place within our consciousness and therefore all others will be compared to that idealistic image.

As we continue to look at the following stories and their related Family Constellation set-ups, a picture will begin to unfold through which a clear demonstration of how we create stories and perceptions that are not based on fact will be revealed. We will go on a journey where the events of the past, when not released, create a "reality" for us today. Let us look again.

Miranda

"The men I fall in love with never fall in love with me"

Payne to Miranda: What would you like to work with today?

Miranda: Relationships. It seems that every time I meet a man and start to have feelings for him or fall in love, he leaves me.

Payne: Has this happened often?

Miranda: More times than I like to think of.

Payne: Have you had any significant relationships in the past?

Miranda: That depends on how you look at it. Significant for me, but it never seems significant to them, they always leave.

Payne: Did anything significant happen in your family of origin? Did any man leave? Your father perhaps, or someone else?

Miranda: No, no one. My parents are still married and there have been no really significant events that I can think of.

Payne: Tell me about the significant men in your life.

Miranda: Well, Bobby was the first, that was when I was at University, then there was Bobby, Charles, Jimmy, Paul and Francis.

Payne: These are all the men you have feelings for, or that you wanted to get serious with?

Miranda: Yes. There have been others, but they were just dates, quite casual relationships.

Payne: Did anything happen that was significant with any of the casual relationships?

Miranda: No. They were just men that I dated, nothing of note.

Payne: OK, well, let us look. Please select a representative for yourself, and one for each of the men you have named: Bobby, Charles, Jimmy, Paul and Francis.

Miranda sets up the constellation. Payne instructs her to place the men in a line and to place her representative opposite them, facing in their direction.

Chapter One – The Stories We Tell

B: Bobby   C: Charles   J: Jimmy   P: Paul   F: Francis
M: Miranda   AC: Aborted Child

Figure 1

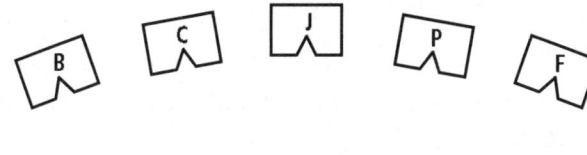

Payne to Miranda's Representative: How are things here when you look at these men?

Miranda's Representative: I can't really look at them, especially the first one.

Payne: Well let's try to look at the first. His name is Bobby.

Miranda's representative lifts her head and looks directly at Bobby.

Payne to Miranda's Representative: How does that feel when you look directly at him?

Miranda's Representative: I feel guilty and I have a slight pain here *(placing her hand on her lower abdomen).*

Payne to Miranda: Is there anything about which you feel guilty with regards to Bobby? Did you have an abortion?

Miranda: Yes, I had an abortion.

Payne to Miranda: What were the circumstances?

Miranda: Well, we were at University together and I got pregnant. I was too young to have a child and I wanted to finish my studies.

Payne to Miranda: And how did Bobby feel about the abortion?

Miranda: He wasn't happy when I had told him that I had an abortion, and we split up.

Payne to Miranda: So you didn't inform him beforehand that you were pregnant and that you were going to have an abortion?

Miranda: No. I thought he may try to convince me to have the baby.

Payne to Miranda: Well, let me work with you directly.

Payne instructs Miranda's representative to sit down and takes Miranda herself directly into the constellation.

Payne to Miranda: Look at Bobby directly.

Miranda: That's difficult to do. I can't really face him.

Payne: Are you able to look at the others?

Miranda: Yes, a little, but it isn't easy. I don't want them to see this.

Payne takes a workshop attendee and places her at Miranda's feet to represent the aborted child.

Figure 2

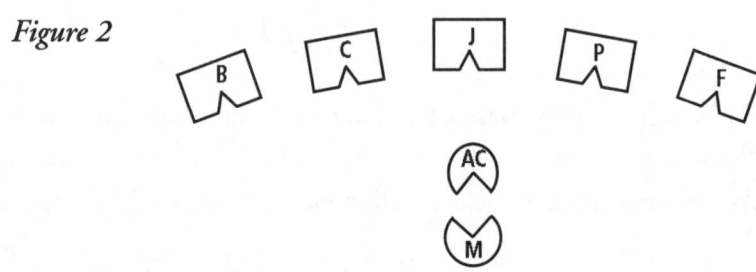

Payne to Miranda: How does that feel with this child at your feet?

Miranda: I feel terrible.

Payne: Please look directly at Bobby and say to him, "This was your child, and I took it away without your consent. I'm deeply sorry for that".

Miranda: "This was your child, and I took it away without your consent. I'm deeply sorry for that". *(Miranda wipes a tear away from her eye.)*

Payne: How does that feel?

Miranda: Not good. But I realize that I've been feeling very guilty. I never told Bobby. I grew up in a period when I strongly believed in a woman's right to choose. I never even considered Bobby's feelings at all, I just did it.

Payne: Now look at the other men, how does that feel?

Miranda: It's difficult. I feel ashamed of myself.

Payne: It would seem that you have been choosing men who would not love you out of some kind of penance.

Miranda: Yes, I see that now. A feeling of not being worthy of love.

Payne: Let's do some more work.

Payne instructs the representatives for all of the men except Bobby to sit down and brings Bobby, Miranda and the aborted child together.

Chapter One – The Stories We Tell

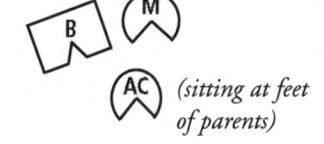

Figure 3   (sitting at feet of parents)

Payne to Bobby: How does that feel?

Bobby: Very sad, and I feel a little angry.

Payne to Miranda: And for you?

Miranda: Not good, I can't really look at either of them.

Payne to Miranda: Please look at Bobby, directly in the eyes, and say to him, "You were my first love and I wronged you deeply".

Miranda to Bobby: You were my first love and I wronged you deeply.

Bobby sheds a tear as he receives Miranda's words.

Payne to Miranda: Now say to him, "I accept the consequences of my actions, please leave it with me".

Miranda to Bobby: I accept the consequences of my actions, please leave it with me.

Payne to Miranda: How is that now?

Miranda: It's heavy, but I have much more clarity. I've always brushed this aside as not being so important. Now I realize that I really did deny Bobby the choice over something very significant; a child.

Payne to Miranda: We're not quite finished.

Miranda: I knew you were going to say that, and this is the bit that's going to be the most difficult.

Payne instructs the representative for the aborted child who is sitting at Bobby's and Miranda's feet to lift her head and look up at her mother.

Payne to Miranda: Please place a hand on your child's head and say the following words, "Beloved child of mine, I am deeply sorry. I now give you a place in my heart where you shall always live".

Miranda: Beloved child of mine, I am deeply sorry. I now give you a place in my heart where you shall always live.

The constellation concludes and Miranda sits next to Payne again.

Payne to Miranda: How do you feel now?

Miranda: Had you asked me directly about this, I would have brushed it off as something of little significance, but now I realize that I have been punishing myself for many years because of this. It answers so many questions.

Payne to Miranda: Now you simply need to give your guilt a proper place and live with it. That doesn't mean that you must now "live as a guilty person", because you've been doing that all along, but it does mean that it needs to be acknowledged and carried with dignity. You see, when we carry our own guilt, we gain strength from it. When we deny it, it becomes a drain for us.

Miranda: So, had I told Bobby, would the abortion have been okay?

Payne: In my experience, there are always consequences for abortions. They go against the natural order of things.

Miranda: So abortions are always wrong?

Payne: I can't comment on that. I don't look at what is right or wrong, I simply look at the consequences of events, decisions and actions. It is not useful to use terms such as right or wrong. However, in my experience, I am yet to work with a woman who has had an abortion for purely social reasons who does not sabotage her life in some way as a sort of penance.

Miranda: It's clear to me now that my guilt about not telling Bobby has made me feel unworthy of being loved by another man, hence I chose men who would reflect that. How do I change this?

Payne: By allowing the work we have just done to sink into your Soul. When you carry your own guilt, there is dignity in that and you will gain strength from it.

Miranda: Do I need to contact Bobby and apologize to him?

Payne: Well, that is up to you. But don't contact him if what you are seeking is forgiveness. Remember, you took choice away from him, and also his child. If you ask for forgiveness, you are then asking him to give you something else after you took so much from him. If you contact him, simply say, "I am deeply sorry, I wronged you", and leave it at that. If you leave it like that, it will be easier for him to forgive you. If you make a story out of it and ask him to forgive you, then you are asking too much, and it won't work. No one can absolve you of this guilt apart from you, and you will gain strength from that.

Conclusion

Miranda started with her story, "The men I fall in love with never fall in love with me", but what was the deeper truth that was revealed? It was apparent that, on investigation of her deeper hidden feelings, she felt guilty about events and decisions in the past. She chose men who would not love her, as a form of self-punishment. When we don't investigate our feelings or the significant events in our lives, we can create stories that have no basis in fact. It may be true that none of the men after Bobby fell in love with her, and, in essence, it is irrelevant. What is relevant are our own perceptions and the stories that lie behind them. Owing to the employment of *the knowing field* in the representational system, we could have investigated further to discover the true feelings of Charles, Jimmy, Paul and Francois; however, of what benefit would that have been to Miranda? The important thing in any investigation is to look at the source; therefore, it was only relevant to work directly with Bobby and the abortion.

A comment on forgiveness

It is very important when we have wronged another that we don't ask for forgiveness, but simply apologise in the simplest way. When we have wronged someone, we have already in a sense taken away something that existed between us, be that love, trust, respect etc. So when we ask for forgiveness, we are asking others to give us something in return, which creates further imbalance.

Chapter Two

EXPRESSING THE LANGUAGE OF THE SOUL

For many, when they first hear of Family Constellation work it sounds like descriptions of psychodrama and role play. However, there are two key elements that differentiate Family Constellation work from other group forms of therapy: firstly, the use of the unseen intelligence of the field and, secondly, the use of healing sentences, the language of the Soul. So how does the use of specific language syntax make such a difference to our healing process? Just as words can be used as weapons and hurt others emotionally, words can also be used for healing. However, there is a little more to it than simply using words. Words alone not only communicate intention, but also energy, as is evident in the field. As we experience within the field of a Family Constellation setup, healing sentences create a perceptible shift in the energy of the entire constellation. But will any sentence create a healing shift if it expresses a truth? In reality, no. The nature of healing sentences needs to be a direct, distilled articulation of a deeper truth – in other words, the sentences need to emanate from the level of the Soul in order to be effective. So how can we know if we are expressing ourselves from our essence, or Soul, or from the level of the personality? The characteristics of communication generated from the level of the personality are defined by superfluous wording and a lack of succinct truth that detracts from the goal of resolution. When the language of the Soul is used, there is more often than not a feeling of "there is no more to say".

Let me give you a brief example regarding marital issues in the context of a family:

"Son, don't get involved in what's going on between your father and me. It really is none of your business. You are far too young and it is none of your concern. I am still your mother and your father is your father, so nothing is really any different".

Or, in the *language of the Soul*:

"Whatever happened between your father and me, leave it with us. We remain your parents".

What we see in Family Constellation work is that such sentences bring greatly needed relief to the children involved, even if those children are adults. The *language of the Soul* sentence above leaves nothing more to be said. It is clear, succinct, and carries the deeper truth that needs to be heard by the child: "We remain your parents".

At times, the deeper truth can at first be difficult for us to accept, especially if what is being expressed goes against what society considers right and proper, or if it is a taboo subject:

"Father, you abused me and hurt me deeply. Because of you my life is a mess and I don't want to be your daughter any longer".

Or, in the *language of the Soul*:

"Dear Father, I allowed it out of love for you. You are still my father, no matter what".

In cases of sexual abuse between a parent and a child, much traditional psychotherapy creates further polarization between parent and child by supporting the child's position as only a victim. What is often missing are two basic truths that are inescapable: the child remains the child of the parent, and the child still loves their parent. Owing to the taboo of incest, undeniable truths are often swept aside in favour of a more punitive stance, which leaves the child (who may now be an adult) in the untenable position of needing to deny their parent. When this is done, not only is forgiveness impossible, but the recovery of innocence for the child also remains at arm's length. The objection to such an approach is usually born out of our need to punish the guilty. What benefit is there to the child if the one that has given them life is punished, especially if the punishing is done by the child through denying their love and their paternity? There is no benefit at all, only further suffering.

How can we consider a sentence like, "Dear Father, I allowed it out of love for you. You are still my father, no matter what", to be the *language of the Soul*? Does the Soul condone such actions and behaviour? No, the Soul neither condones nor rejects any action; it simply acknowledges what is, and it deals with simple truths. So let us look at the sentence more closely:

"I allowed it out of love for you".

What does it mean when we say that? Is it true? A child naturally loves its life-giver, even when that parent is abusive in any and all forms. Children have

Chapter Two – Expressing the Language of the Soul

an innocent love for their parents that is unconditional in nature, so when sexual abuse takes place, that innocent unconditional love is still present. When we say, "I allowed it out of love for you", we are once again reconnected to that unconditional love and therefore our shame begins to recede and we once again regain our innocence. This, however, does not let the perpetrator off the hook; they remain with their guilt and the consequences of their actions. When we seek punitive measures or consequences, we imprison the child in shame. In Family Constellation work, we become aware of three basic principles: there is that which is our own business and our own fate, there is that which belongs to another and has nothing to do with us, and there is that which belongs purely to fate, or a greater force that we cannot challenge (wars, for example). Therefore, the fate of the father in such cases is not the business of the child, even though the child has been a victim to the parent's perpetration of sexual abuse. A very usual response is to think, "Well of course it is the child's business, he/she was hurt by this!" What we must ask ourselves is the following: Of what benefit is it to the child to be involved in the consequences for the father? There are none, only a societal need to punish the "bad" ones that has never really served anyone. It has often been said that an eye for an eye simply leads to us becoming blind.

"You are still my father, no matter what".

Would the child exist without a father? The simple answer is no, he/she would not. Therefore, "no matter what, you are still my father". Her paternity is an undeniable fact, it cannot be undone. As we have seen through Family Constellation work, much positive energy that supports us comes to us from our ancestors: grandparents, great-grandparents and so on and so forth. There is a wealth of both life force energy and experience that is handed down to us at conception. When we deny our paternity, or either one of our parents, we sever ties to our ancestors. This is most often the cause of disruptive life patterns, even illness.

The *language of the Soul* in such cases does not seek to deny that wrong was done, nor does it seek to deny that it was a terrible thing. However, it highlights the undeniable truths that have been overlooked in such situations owing to the pain and shame of sexual abuse, thereby offering relief from those feelings. When we are able to express the depth of love that still exists, healing can take place. It is true to say that love conquers all, but in a society that strongly frowns upon incest in any shape or form, it often takes great courage to go against the grain and express love for one's abuser.

So how can we apply the *language of the Soul* to many of life's situations? Let us take a look at some examples of client stories I have dealt with, many of which are very common in human relationships:

Norma
"I was abused by my aunt"

Payne: What would you like to work with?

Norma: This is very difficult for me. I originally came to the workshop with another issue in mind, but after the last constellation (that dealt with sexual abuse), it is right on the surface and I can't run away from it, even though I want to.

Payne: What happened?

Norma: I was abused by my aunt when I was little girl.

Payne: Did it continue over a period of time, or was it a single incident?

Norma: No, it happened on a fairly continuous basis over a few years. It started when I was about three or four years old.

Payne: What were the circumstances?

Norma: Well, we were a poor family and my parents lived with my mother's parents and also her sister, my aunt. We all lived in one house.

Payne: So you lived with your aunt?

Norma: Yes.

Payne: And how old was your aunt at the time of the abuse?

Norma: About 18 or 19.

Payne: So she was merely a child, too, in many respects. One wonders where she learnt this behaviour.

Norma: Well, I've since learnt that my grandfather abused all of the girls in the family, although my mother won't speak of it.

Payne: Well, let's set up a constellation. Choose representatives for yourself, your mother, your aunt and your grandfather. We may need your father a little later, but we'll start with this. Your grandfather is your mother's father, is that correct?

Norma: Yes, we lived with my mother's parents.

Norma selects representatives from the workshop to represent her grandfather, mother, aunt and herself and places them according to her feeling in a standing position on the workshop floor.

Chapter Two – Expressing the Language of the Soul

GF: Grandfather   A: Aunt   M: Mother   N: Norma

Figure 1

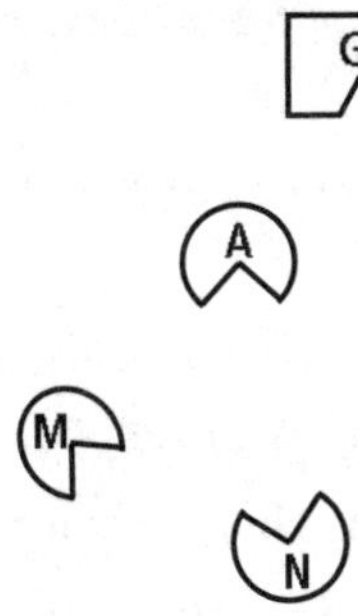

Payne observes the setup of the constellation and notices that the representative for Norma's aunt is looking very distressed.

Payne to Aunt: How are things here?

Aunt: I am overwhelmed with shame, grief and a lot of fear. I am very uncomfortable with my father behind me.

Payne to Norma's Representative: How are things here?

Norma's Representative: I can't look up at anyone. I don't want to look at my aunt, and I don't like my grandfather standing there. This is very uncomfortable.

Payne to Grandfather: How are things with you?

Grandfather: I feel aggressive plus I have this "couldn't give a damn" attitude. I look down on them.

Payne to Mother: How are things with you?

Mother: I just don't want to be here. I can't look at anyone.

Payne walks slowly back over to Norma's representative and gently places a hand on her lower back.

Payne to Norma's Representative: Please look up at your aunt, even if it's difficult.

Norma's representative begins to sob as she gently lifts up her head to look directly at her aunt.

Payne to Norma's Representative: How is that now?

Norma's Representative: I'm very sad and it is much easier to look at her than I thought it would be. I'm overwhelmed with sadness and I'm sad for her.

The Language of the Soul

The two women, Norma's representative and the representative for Norma's aunt look across the space between them at one another. Both have tears flowing down their faces.

Payne to Norma's Representative: Let us try and bring the two of you closer together, shall we?

Payne slowly brings the two women together. They immediately embrace and sob with one another.

Payne to Mother: How is this for you? (She is visibly crying.)

Mother: My heart is aching, but I feel some relief that they are embracing like that.

Payne replaces Norma's representative with the client Norma in the constellation. Norma, sobbing, stands in front of her aunt's representative, not yet embracing her.

Payne to Norma: How is it to stand directly in front of your young aunt like this?

Norma: Not as difficult as I thought. I feel very sad.

Payne to Norma: Please say to your aunt, "Beloved Aunt, I allowed it out of love for you".

Norma could not utter the words owing to her tears and lunged forward, embracing her aunt, and the two sobbed together whilst holding one another.

Payne to Norma: Look up into your aunt's eyes and try to say the words.

Norma: I allowed it out of love for you, dear Aunt.

Payne: How is that now?

Norma: It is such a relief. I don't resent her any longer, and I know that I love her. It feels good. I think she suffered too.

The representative for Norma's mother moves spontaneously over towards her sister and daughter and the three women embrace and sob together.

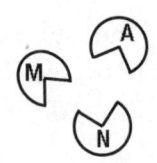

Figure 2

Chapter Two – Expressing the Language of the Soul

Payne to Norma: Do you feel resolved with your aunt?

Norma: Yes, and it's a great relief. I've been working on this for many years and I thought it was resolved. I never imagined that I had these feelings of love towards her.

Payne: As a 19-year-old brought up in an abusive home, your aunt was really nothing more than a child, so also innocent in many ways. We'll return to the subject of your grandfather at some later stage. Just allow this constellation to move into your Soul and let it work for you. This journey will be one step at a time.

Norma: Thank you. I think there is a lot to clear with my mother and grandfather but, as you said, not today.

Conclusion

In this case, it is clear that Norma loved her aunt and looking at the broader picture of the grandfather's involvement made it much easier for Norma to speak the language of her own Soul: "Beloved Aunt, I allowed it out of love for you". How true would this be if the abuser was not an aunt, uncle, brother, father or sister? In my observation, in the vast majority of cases, this sentiment still holds true.

Let us look now at some work we did with Sandra.

Sandra

"My relationships with men simply don't work"

Payne to Sandra: What would you like to work with today?

Sandra: My relationships with men simply don't work; as soon as they get close, I sabotage the relationship.

Payne: What is the feeling?

Sandra: I just can't get close to them; I get afraid.

Payne: Have there been any significant events in your life?

Sandra: Yes, I was molested when I was younger.

Payne: By whom?

Sandra: A family friend, a friend of my parents.

Payne: Shall we work with this directly and see where it takes us?

The Language of the Soul

Sandra: Yes, but I have a lot of conflict around this subject, and I feel ashamed because of my feelings.

Payne: Please explain.

Sandra: I love this man. I know what he did was wrong because I was only a little girl, but he was a friend and I feel fondness for him. *(Sandra sobs)* I'm not supposed to have feelings like that. It is not that I think it was OK what he did, but I loved him anyway and still have feelings for him.

Payne: In a sense, he was your first love.

Sandra: Yes, he was, but I feel so conflicted and guilty.

Payne selects one of the male workshop participants to stand in as a representative for Sandra's molester. The representative stands directly in front of where Sandra and Payne are sitting in the workshop.

S: Sandra A: Abuser M: Mother

Figure 1

Payne to Sandra: Just look at him and let's see what comes up for you.

Payne leaves Sandra in silence as she gazes at the representative for the family friend who molested her.

Payne: What happens?

Sandra: Such a mixture of feelings. I'm angry at him. I feel guilty and I also feel love for him. It's all mixed into one. I feel so conflicted.

Payne: Why do you suppose that you feel guilty?

Sandra: I feel guilty because I love him and I'm not supposed to.

Payne: That is true, but there is also a deeper truth. When we either dehumanise someone we love or try to deny a love that exists, the Soul cannot tolerate that, and so guilt follows. How would you feel if you told your mother that you love him?

Sandra: That would be very difficult.

Payne addresses the group present:

This is the problem when western Christian cultures seek to polarize individuals into being either "good" or "bad" and prescribes punitive actions to rectify such matters. Of what benefit is this to Sandra or to any victim of sexual abuse? They feel conflicted and that conflict in itself is the

Chapter Two – Expressing the Language of the Soul

harbinger of the emotional wound. No one is condoning the behaviour of the perpetrators; however, the essential question is, of what benefit is it to the victim when they are expected to deny the natural bond that exists between them and their perpetrator?

Payne: Let us now take a representative for your mother.

Payne has the representative for Sandra's mother stand in front of them, standing to one side of Sandra's abuser.

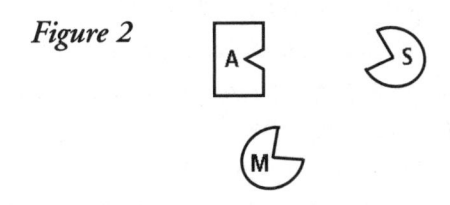

Figure 2

Payne to Sandra: Look at your mother and say to her, "I allowed it out of love for him, he was a family friend".

Sandra: I allowed it out of love for him, he was a family friend.

Payne: How did that feel?

Sandra: It was very difficult to say, not because it isn't true, but because I feel that I'm not allowed to say that.

Payne: Let's see if you can say the same thing to him, "I allowed it out of love for you".

Sandra utters the words, moves across to her abuser and flings her arms around him. They embrace and sob together.

Payne to Sandra: In many ways, this man was your first love. When a first love relationship is not resolved, it makes it very difficult for us to form successful relationships in the future. You see, we don't allow ourselves to have these feelings for our abuser as society condemns such actions and therefore also the feelings. However, societal condemnation or not, we cannot deny that the feelings exist. Even as a little girl, you loved this man and now that you can acknowledge it, you regain your innocence. This kind of love that you have for him is very innocent, and it is quite exquisite. However, this does not mean that the same applies to him. It is a different matter altogether for him, but he is not the subject of our focus today, you are.

Sandra: I feel relieved. I've finally been able to give a voice to these feelings that I've felt ashamed of for so long. I can also let go of him now.

Conclusion

In Sandra's case, her abuser was a family friend. Those who are loved and trusted by parents, are also loved and trusted by children; therefore the healing sentence, "I allowed it out of love for you", still holds true in most cases. However, it can also be that the child says to the mother or father, "I allowed it out of loyalty to you", meaning that the child offers themselves up as a victim out of loyalty to their parent's friendship with the abuser. In a sense, they are saying to their parents, "I allowed it out of love for you".

What is important to re-emphasize here, is that this approach to healing sexual abuse through expressions of the Soul in no way lets the abuser off the hook. The abuser still carries their fate which is no one else's responsibility but their own. We say that, however, in a respectful manner, not in a punitive manner. When we understand the energetic and trans-generational impact of such actions, we must also know that the families and children of perpetrators also share in the fate. Would we want to bear malice towards them? Or would we bow respectfully to the fate that has been handed them? Would the distilled truth of "I allowed it out of love for you" still be true if the abuser is not a family friend or a member of the family? In the case of stepfathers, it still holds true, but what about a complete stranger or a violent attack that leads to rape? Let us look.

Julie
"*I was raped*"

Payne to Julie: What would you like to work with?

Julie: Several years ago my home was burgled and the intruder raped me in my bed. Even years later, I still feel that I'm holding onto him in some way.

Payne: Well, let's keep this simple. Please select a representative for yourself and one for the rapist and place them in a standing position within the workshop floor space.

Chapter Two – Expressing the Language of the Soul

R: The Rapist   J: Julie   F: Rapist's Father   M: Rapist's Mother

Figure 1

Payne: I've noticed that you've placed him in the corner, as a far away as possible. But let me take a look and see what transpires.

Payne walks into the constellation. The tension in the "field" is very palpable.

Payne to Julie's Representative: How are things here?

Julie: OK. *(She has her hand folded over her stomach.)*

Payne: And how do you feel when you look at this man standing over there?

Julie's Representative: Fine. He is where he should be. *(Julie's representative's body language expresses some aggression, defiance and superiority towards the rapist.)*

Payne walks over to the rapist's representative and turns him around to face Julie's representative and slowly guides him across the room to stand in front of Julie, about 2 metres away.

Payne to Julie's Representative: How does that feel now?

Julie's Representative: I'm shaking with anger.

Payne to Julie's Representative: Say to him, "You are not human and I exclude you".

Julie's Representative: Um…I thought that would be really easy to say, it was what I was feeling, but I can't say it.

Payne: You are unable to say it because it goes against the nature of the Soul which is inclusive of all things.

Payne replaces the representative with Julie herself.

Payne to Julie: How does that feel to stand opposite him?

Julie: In the chair I felt defiant, just like the representative. I also thought it would be easy for her to say those words and I felt it when it became difficult for her.

Payne: Well, let us look at an even truer picture.

Payne takes representatives for the rapist's parents and stands them behind him.

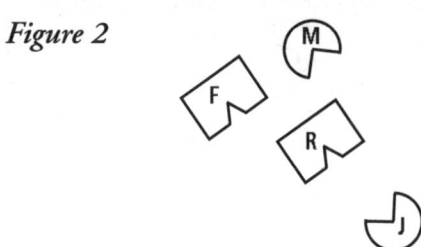

Figure 2

Payne to Rapist: How does that feel?

Rapist: I also felt a little defiant in the beginning, feeling stronger and bigger than her. When you brought in my parents I suddenly felt weak and ashamed.

Payne to Julie: How does that feel for you when you see him standing there with his parents?

Julie: I see that he is a man, he has become more human in my eyes. I almost feel sorry for him.

Payne: I notice that your nose turns slightly upwards when you say that. Why don't you say, "I'm a better human being than you'll ever be", to him.

Julie: No, I can't say that.

Payne: It would seem that all these years you have only realized what he did to you, which is natural. However, can you see what he has done to himself?

Julie: I'm beginning to.

Payne: Say this to him, "I see that you are heavily burdened by this, and I give you a place in my heart".

Julie: I see that you are heavily burdened by this, and I give you a place in my heart.

Payne: How was that?

Julie: It was a relief. I feel freer.

Payne: Now try this: "I see clearly that your family is burdened by this, and that is a heavy fate. I wish you and your family well".

Julie: I see clearly that your family is burdened by this, and that is a heavy fate. I wish you and your family well.

Payne: And how does that feel?

Julie: I no longer feel superior to him, he's human just like me and we both have a burden to heal.

Julie spontaneously crosses over to the rapist and embraces him. At this point she understands deeply that they are both equal in their wound and shows him loving affection.

Conclusion

The pivotal point of this constellation is when Julie realizes that the burden of the rapist is equal to her own. How does a Soul carry actions such as rape? Or how does any perpetrator carry their deeds? The answer is, heavily. When Julie was able to grasp the consequences for his family, she was suddenly able to see him as human once more. Until that point, Julie would have been condemned to feel guilt and shame, feeling all the time that these feelings only derived from the rape itself. However, what we see clearly is that the Soul cannot endure holding such feelings of superiority towards another human being, so guilt ensues. It is only through a sense of equality that we can find any sense of relief or complete resolution.

In this constellation, the healing sentence, "I allowed it out of love for you", is not relevant. The rapist was neither a family member nor a family friend, therefore the healing sentence does not play a part in this scenario; however, love does play a part. On the realization not only of the rapist's burden, but also of the burden to his family (and possible children), Julie was able to bridge the gap between resentment and grace, and move into a place of forgiveness – *not* as the good forgiving the bad, but as one human being acknowledging the burden of another and recognizing that such incidents do not stand in isolation but impact entire family systems, and not just her own.

The expression of the Soul is, *I see clearly that your family is burdened by this, and that is a heavy fate.*

That is distilled, un-escapable truth; it simply acknowledges what is. Whenever we are stuck on letting something go, or on forgiving someone for a transgression, no matter how severe, it simply means that we have lost greater clarity and the ability to see things as they really are. Julie's rapist now has a fate and he must endure the consequences of that.

Another Soul-filled movement that can be made is to both inwardly and outwardly bow to the fate of the rapist with deep respect. He and his family will carry this burden for many years, and perhaps his family for generations.

Do we wish his children ill? Or do we give them a place in our hearts as well? When we express the language of the Soul, we free ourselves from the clutter of our imprisoning stories about what we think is true. Yes, it is true that Julie was raped, that is not up for debate. However, the clutter that imprisoned Julie was her perception that her rapist is not human, perhaps having no Soul at all. Each of us inherits a fate when we perpetrate such actions – perhaps prison, perhaps capital punishment, or perhaps no judicial punishment at all, but simply the burden of guilt that we carry and the consequences for the generations that follow. It is a heavy fate and, guilty or innocent, the Soul respects fate.

When we express the *language of the Soul*, we touch essence. When we touch essence, we are liberated. It is said that "the truth shall set you free". The *language of the Soul* is that truth and it is the key to freedom from emotional burdens.

That which is hidden will always come to light

During a training evening, one of my male students was asked to represent a gay man in a constellation. As the constellation finished, he started making overtly stereotypical gay gestures; standing limp-wristed, lisping and generally behaving in a demeaning way. I pointed out to him that he had never felt the need to mock anyone he had represented previously and that his behaviour was not only disrespectful to the "field" and family Soul, but also to gay people in general. The discussion continued over the next few days via email and by telephone and the conversation gradually turned around to the subject of his last constellation. This particular student, who has gracefully given me permission to write his story, has been working on the issues of his violent tendencies, which at times have led him to black out just before assaulting someone. Two of his constellations revealed that much of his anger was inherited from his father and that his father had most probably been subjected to teasing, and probably sexual abuse, whilst in a boarding school for boys. Together we decided that we would look at the issue of his father and the boarding school again, as we both felt that his disrespect for gay men was in some way linked to this.

Chapter Two – Expressing the Language of the Soul

Steve
"My father's boarding school"

Steve: I've had so much food for thought since the incident the other evening, and I am perplexed. I work in a creative industry and I have had many gay colleagues over the years. Since you pointed out that I've mocked gay stereotypes on more than one occasion, I believe that there is something there and I want to look at it. It feels out of character to behave in such ways.

Payne: In your last constellation, it was very clear that you have carried some of your father's feelings in connection with his time in boarding school. What seems to be more than a coincidence is that whenever the subject of male-on-male sexual abuse has come up in the public workshops, you have always been chosen as a representative, even though plenty of other males have been present. I think that we need to look at this subject more directly again, would you agree?

Steve: Yes, I agree. Many things seem to be inter-linked with this issue.

Payne: Let's start in a simple way. Select a representative for your father and the boarding school and place them according to your feeling.

Boarding School

F: Father   S: Steve   BS: Boarding School

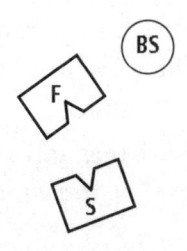

As I placed Steve in a standing position opposite his father and the boarding school, Steve falls to his knees, breathing rapidly, as if in the middle of re-living a trauma.

Payne to Steve: What's happening?

Steve: It's unbearable.

Payne to Steve: What happens if you look at your father's boarding school?

Steve: Mostly aggression, I can barely look at it.

Payne to Father's Representative: What happens if you look at the boarding school?

Father: I can't look there.

Payne takes a representative for Steven's grandfather and places him behind Steven's father for support.

Payne to Father: How is that now?

Father: Much better, I feel stronger.

Payne to Steven: How does that feel now with your grandfather behind your father?

Steven: Much calmer.

Payne to Father: Please look at the boarding school directly and tell me what happens.

Father: I feel great shame and anger. It is still a little too much to look at it directly.

Payne to Steven: How are things now?

Steven: It is difficult for me to stand up and I still can't look directly at anyone.

Payne to Steven: Please look up at your father and say to him, "I'm ashamed of you".

Steven breaks down in tears and his rapid, heavy breathing starts again.

Steven: You hit the nail on the head. I've always felt ashamed of my father and I've never understood why. I've just hidden the feeling for many years. It was always a mystery to me.

Payne to Steven: So look at your father and say to him, "Dear Father, I've carried this shame out of love for you". *(Steven sobs loudly as he utters these words.)*

Payne to Father: Please say to your son, "Dear Son, leave the boarding school with me, it has nothing to do with you, and I am still your father, no matter what happened".

Father: "Dear Son, leave the boarding school with me, it has nothing to do with you, and I am still your father, no matter what happened".

Payne to Father: How does that feel?

Father: I feel great love for my son, and also I am very serious when I say that he should leave it with me, it really has nothing to do with him.

Chapter Two – Expressing the Language of the Soul

Payne to Steven: Now say to your father, "I take you as my father and I respectfully leave the boarding school with you".

After Steven says the words, father and son embrace lovingly and Steven reports feeling relieved to have gained his father in a new way and left his entanglement with the events in the boarding school behind.

In this example, the language of the Soul is powerful with two expressions:

"I take you as my father".

and

"I've carried this shame out of love for you".

Why would these sentences carry so much power? The heterosexual victims of homosexual rape or sexual abuse often feel that they have been feminised in some way and therefore have lost their right to call themselves "men".

In saying, "I've carried this shame out of love for you", Steven was able to feel how he had been carrying, on a much deeper level, his father's own shame in connection with events that took place in the boarding school. In addition, he was able to see more clearly his need to shame gay men in order to compensate for the general feeling between himself and his father that they in some way did not fully earn the right to belong to the world of men. The healing sentence, "I take you as my father", is pivotal in healing this collective shame. As Steven's father had felt deep shame, Steven was unable to take his father fully as his father. He had spent many years acting out his father's shame and rage through acts of aggression. As Steven "took" his father, he was able to become the son, and finally leave the shame where it belonged.

The main difference between much psychotherapeutic practice and utilizing the *language of the Soul* is that the latter approach is devoid of story; it focuses in on the heart of the matter with pin-point accuracy. Steven could have spent months, if not years, talking to a professional about his feelings of anger, rage, shame and the resulting aggression. Often, during a Family Constellation set-up, use can be made of sentences that appear to be the opposite of the healing we want to achieve. For example, when I asked Steven to say, "I'm ashamed of you", the purpose behind the sentence was to reveal the truth of a feeling, to simply place a precise focus on the issue at hand. What this revealed in Steven's case was the shame felt in the family system that could be attributed to his father's past experiences in the boarding school. So can such sentences be considered the *language of the Soul*? As such statements acknowledge what is, in an undeniable manner, they can indeed be considered the *language of the Soul* as they reveal the "illness" devoid of story. Such sentences are only truly effective when delivered in a controlled and focused manner. If we were to allow the client to verbalise their feelings, the likelihood is that a long story would be told, only serving to muddy the waters and create a lack of focus. We would simply find ourselves talking in circles and returning to where we started with no clear resolution found.

Of what use, then, would sentences such as, "I am ashamed of you", be outside of the context of a Family Constellation? In Family Constellation work we employ the "field" and representatives that offer the facilitator information regarding the true story with great accuracy. Can the *language of the Soul* still be effective without such powerful tools? In short, the answer is yes.

A client can be guided to uncover his or her own feelings in a very controlled manner which will have the same level of focus and therefore similar benefits. As human beings, we often feel obliged to find logical reasons behind our feelings. Therefore, in Steven's case, he would start with, "I feel ashamed of my father because…", at which point we launch full-steam into a story that may be rather long. These stories satisfy our logical mind's need to understand the "why", but they do little in terms of providing a healing resolution. On an individual basis, we can simply sit with such sentences and say no more until another clearly-defined feeling surfaces, such as, "I feel ashamed of myself". This can then be left in silence until the next feeling comes, which may be, "I feel that I'm not worthy of the world of men". At this point, we can investigate if these statements are in actuality true. Steven's father is a man, and Steven himself is a man, so is the statement, "I feel that I'm not worthy of the world of men" true? Indeed, it is not. At this point, I must acknowledge the work of Byron Katie who has done much work to assist individuals in a similar way to remove themselves from their stories and look at distilled truth in a comparable manner. As many of the feelings we have are linked to events within the family system and to hidden loyalties, most of us have great difficulty in finding any resolution to such feelings, so we create stories to fit the feeling. It is the nature of the mind to do so. However, in Family Constellation work, we go beyond the mind into the family Soul and the energetic connections that exist between family members and extend to our ancestors.

Chapter Two – Expressing the Language of the Soul

The key to expressing the *language of the Soul* is to become quiet. Part of the training that my students go through is to learn the skill of moving into the "void" when they enter the "field" of a Family Constellation. We are so accustomed to trying to figure things out logically. With all the mind chatter that goes along with that, the "void" can feel like quite an uncomfortable place. Within the void is everything and nothing simultaneously. As we enter "nothing", everything becomes available to us in a very clear, concise and undeniable way. The full benefits of the *language of the Soul* can only be harvested when we are willing to "not know" and not have answers to anything at all. The mind seeks to know, and what it doesn't understand, it will rationalize, even to the extent of creating a story that is neither true nor very helpful. As we choose peace over the need to be right, the *language of the Soul* comes to us more clearly.

Let us now look at a very common situation and see how the *language of the Soul* can assist.

Cheryl
"I have difficulty with my husband's first wife"

Payne: What would you like to work with?

Cheryl: I have great difficulty with my husband's first wife.

Payne: Does he have children with her?

Cheryl: Yes, two, a boy and a girl. They are nine and twelve years old.

Payne: So what is the issue for you?

Cheryl: She seems to demand a lot of his time and I really don't like it when he goes to see her.

Payne: Is he going to see her, or his children?

Cheryl: Well, both. The children don't really want to meet at our house.

Payne instructs Cheryl to select representatives for herself, her husband and her husband's first wife.

FW: First wife   H: Husband   C: Cheryl

Figure 1

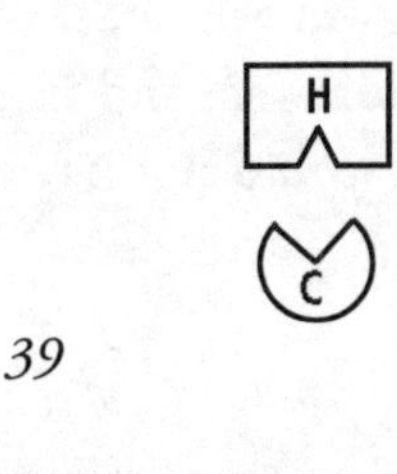

Payne to First Wife: How are things here?

First wife: I'm angry, I don't like the way I've been placed.

Payne to Husband: How are things here?

Husband: Also irritated. I feel confrontational with my wife, and I feel irritated that my first wife was placed facing the corner.

Payne turns the first wife around so she now faces her husband and her husband's second wife.

Payne to Cheryl's Representative: How are things with you now?

Cheryl's Representative: Not comfortable, I don't like that she is looking at him and facing inwards.

Payne to Cheryl's Representative: Well, he is the father of her children, doesn't she have the right to look at him?

Cheryl's representative does not answer and simply folds her arms over her solar plexus.

Payne to Husband: Please say to your second wife whilst gesturing towards your first wife, "This is the mother of my children, and together we will always be the parents".

Husband: This is the mother of my children, and together we will always be the parents.

Payne to Cheryl: How does that feel now?

Cheryl: I don't like it at all, even though it is true.

Payne to Cheryl: Please look at your husband's first wife and say to her, "You were the first, I am only the second".

Cheryl: I don't want to say that.

Payne: But it is the truth, you are only the second and she is the mother of his children. That must be respected. When you compete to be in first place, you cannot win, but as you submit to being in second place, you will become elevated in their eyes, and in the eyes of the children. Why do you suppose that the children do not wish to visit your home? Children will always sense when their mother is not respected, so out of loyalty to her, they will not come to your home. No one needs to say anything, it is simply felt in that way. Now say to her, "You came before me, and thank you for making space for me, for without that, I would not have this wonderful man".

Chapter Two – *Expressing the Language of the Soul*

Cheryl: "You came before me, and thank you for making space for me, for without that, I would not have this wonderful man".

Payne: How does that feel now?

Cheryl: Better. I can see that she has given me a gift by leaving.

Payne: As the second wife, you need to submit to the fact that your husband will always be bonded to this woman, even when he loves you. Their children bind them. In the future, there may be weddings for the children, grandchildren, birthdays, christenings and other celebrations. Can you imagine that he would not attend? Of course he will. And what is best for the children? What is best is that he attends such events with their mother at his side.

Payne takes two representatives to stand in for the children.

Figure 2

Payne to Cheryl: Now face the mother again and say to her, "You are the first, I am just the second, and I honour you as the mother of my husband's children", and bow your head to her as you complete the sentence.

Cheryl: You are the first, I am just the second, and I honour you as the mother of my husband's children.

Payne: How does that feel now?

Cheryl: Surprisingly good, the tension has gone.

Payne to the Children: How does that feel to you?

Son: Relieved, I feel relaxed now. It was a little tense before.

Daughter: Very good. I like her (Cheryl), but it was difficult before she said that to my mother.

Payne: And how is the father doing?

Husband: I couldn't be happier. All the tension has gone.

Payne to Cheryl: Just look at your husband for a moment, do you notice how he is radiating and smiling towards you?

Cheryl: *(Wiping a tear from her eye)* Yes, it feels wonderful!

Payne to Cheryl: You see, when you take your rightful place, which is second, you become elevated in everyone's eyes. You cannot compete with this woman and you cannot deny her rightful place as the first. Second marriages often fall apart for this very reason. When you marry someone who already has children, you need to be aware, and accept, that from day one you will only be the second. When you are not threatened by that, and you honour the mother or father of the children from the first marriage, your own marriage will be secure.

Conclusion

In this example, the *language of the Soul* is a statement of what is. When a couple has children, they are bonded for life. This needs to be taken into consideration by the new couple. What is important to the children needs to be acknowledged. Children, no matter their age, feel more secure when they see their parents together, even when they are divorced and new marriages have been entered into. Children will invariably be loyal to the parent that is least respected. In this case, the children were loyal to their mother as Cheryl had not afforded her the respect that was due. This scenario commonly causes tension in second marriages when the new spouse has a defensive stance towards the first spouse. We cannot underestimate the bond of loyalty that exists between couples that have had children together, even when on the surface they do not seem to get along.

The healing sentence, "You came before me, and thank you for making space for me, for without that, I would not have this wonderful man", acknowledges the gift that was given as a result of the first couple separating. It is important for each of us to acknowledge the role that previous partners have had in handing us the gift of our current partner.

When children are involved, if the first spouse and parent of the children is not honoured, we create tension within our new relationship. In Cheryl's case, as she did not honour the mother and first wife, she was in effect disrespecting her husband's children, and tension in her marriage ensued. When the mother is not respected, then Cheryl's message to the children is, "I dishonour the part of your mother I see alive in you". This is something that the father, her husband, could not tolerate, whether consciously or not.

The healing sentence, "You are the first, I am just the second, and I honour you as the mother of my husband's children", is firstly a statement of

Chapter Two – Expressing the Language of the Soul

what is; it is an undeniable truth. Secondly, it honours the mother as being an inseparable part of Cheryl's husband. As Cheryl bows to her place of "being only the second", she becomes elevated in everyone else's eyes. When we seek to compete with a previous spouse or partner for first place when in fact we are not first, we can never succeed and only tensions will arise. As we submit to the truth of what is, our place and position within the new family system is automatically elevated. It really makes no difference at all if our new partner professes to love us more than the first because the hierarchy of firsts and seconds still exists and still needs to be honoured.

In this case study, the *language of the Soul* is a clear statement of undeniable truth. When we acknowledge what is, tension dissipates, and this is the healing power of this approach.

Sean
"I love him, but it's so difficult"

Payne: What would you like to work with?

Sean: I've been in a gay relationship for five years and we very often reach the verge of splitting up. I love my partner very much and I don't want to lose him.

Payne: Had either of you had significant relationships before meeting one another?

Sean: No, just dating and casual boyfriends, nothing really serious for either of us. We met in our late twenties. I'm now 32 and Gavin is 34.

Payne: Can you tell me a little about your family of origin?

Sean: I am the second child of four children. My father has always had great difficulty accepting that I am gay. Even my mother did at first, too.

Payne: Do they acknowledge Gavin as your partner?

Sean: No, not really. They are polite to him, but it is not as if Gavin is their "son-in-law".

Payne: And Gavin's family?

Sean: They are very good with us. We always get invited to family functions and Gavin's sister always refers to me as her "brother-in-law", which makes me feel very welcome.

Payne: It sounds very nice to me. So why do the two of you reach the verge of splitting up so often?

Sean: It's me, I often withdraw, and I don't know why.

Payne: Well, let us look at this directly. Please select representatives for yourself, your parents, Gavin and his parents, and let's see what emerges.

Sean takes representatives form the workshop and places them according to his inner feeling in standing positions on the workshop floor.

GF: Gavin's Father GM: Gavin's Mother G: Gavin SF: Sean's Father
SM: Sean's Mother S: Sean GrM: Sean's Grandmother
GrF: Sean's Grandfather GGF: Sean's Great Grandfather
GGGF: Sean's Great Great Grandfather

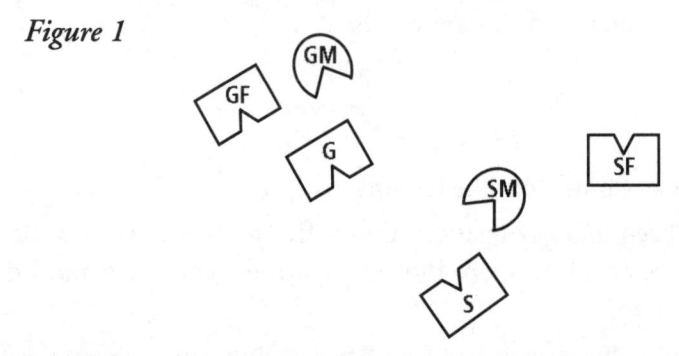

Figure 1

Payne: What is clear is that your parents don't stand behind you, and that's difficult. Let me investigate further.

Payne to Sean's Father: How are things here?

Sean's Father: Quite fine, I'm happy here. I would prefer it if my wife was next to me.

Payne to Sean's Mother: How are things here?

Sean's mother: Difficult. I feel my husband is over there and I want to go to him, but my son is right here. I feel torn, it's not comfortable.

Payne to Gavin's Representative: How are things here?

Gavin's Representative: I feel supported, but when I look at him (Sean's representative), I feel a little weak. But I also feel the bond with him, love. It's kind of difficult.

Payne to Sean's Representative: How are things here?

Sean's Representative: I feel a longing for him (Gavin), but I feel something like a magnetic pull behind me and I feel weak.

Chapter Two – Expressing the Language of the Soul

Payne walks over to the representative for Sean's father and turns him around to face the constellation.

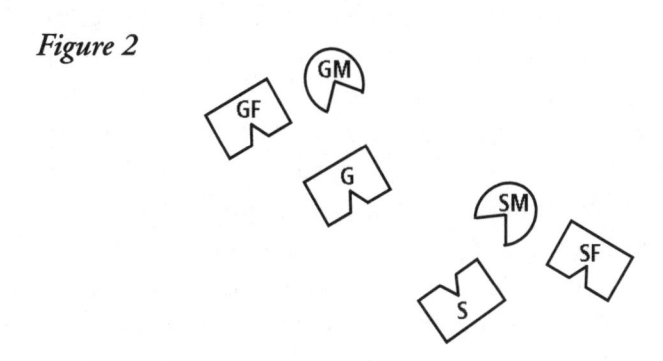

Figure 2

Payne to Sean's Father: How is that now?

Sean's Father: I don't really want to look there, it is difficult.

Payne to Sean's Representative: Say to Gavin, "It's difficult without my father behind me".

Sean's Representative: It's difficult without my father behind me.

Payne: How does that feel when you say that?

Sean's Representative: It's true, and I feel a deep sense of shame, like I'm not good enough either for my father or for him (Gavin).

Payne turns to Sean, the client.

Payne to Sean: How is it for you to hear this?

Sean: *(Moved to tears)* It's true. I feel that I don't belong to anyone and that I'm just not good enough for Gavin.

Payne to Gavin's Representative: How was it for you when Sean said, "It's difficult without my father behind me"?

Gavin's Representative: It's true, and it is difficult for me. It is like I have to give too much – almost replace his father.

Comment: When the healing sentence, "It's difficult without my father behind me", is spoken, it brings into focus the real underlying issue in the relationship between Gavin and Sean. Even though it is evident that there is a bond of love between them, Sean feels weakened by not having his father stand behind him. This creates a drain of energy for Gavin, as he feels that he needs to "give too much" in order to compensate for the lack of support from Sean's father. In this way,

The Language of the Soul

despite the bond of love between the two men, there is an imbalance that is taking its toll on the relationship. Gavin cannot be anything more than a partner in a spousal relationship. Trying to compensate for the lack of support from Sean's father is too high a price. This particular constellation highlights, in my view, why so many gay and lesbian couples find it difficult to sustain long-term relationships. When a father turns away from his gay son (or daughter), the son feels shamed. Within that shame he often does not feel worthy of a true life partner and will often turn away from the men that profess their love to him. In order for a man to feel strong and secure in himself, he has a deep need to belong to his father and to the male line, irrespective of his sexual orientation. When he feels that he does not belong, he is weakened by this, which in turn creates a strain on his long-term relationships. Let us continue:

Payne to Sean's Representative: Please turn and look at your father. How does it feel when you look at him?

Sean's Representative: It's difficult. He looks stern.

Payne to Father: How does it feel now that your son is looking at you?

Father: It's difficult. I feel cold towards him.

Payne takes a male representative to stand in for Sean's grandfather and places him right behind Sean's father.

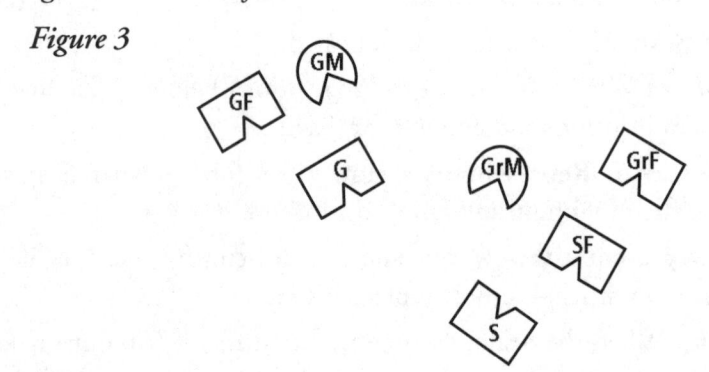

Figure 3

Payne to Father: How does that feel with your father behind you?

Father: The same. Cold.

Payne to Father: Please turn and look at your father. How does that feel when you look at him?

Chapter Two – Expressing the Language of the Soul

Figure 4

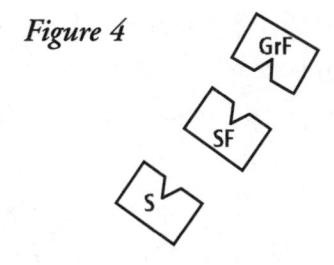

Father: Nothing. Nothing at all. Perhaps a little intimidated by him.

Payne to Grandfather: How does that feel to look at your son?

Grandfather: Also nothing, except that I feel much bigger than him.

Payne to Father: Please say to your father, "Father, please be gentle with me".

Father: That's difficult to say. It's like I am not allowed to say that.

Payne: Please just try to say the words.

Father: Father, please be gentle with me. *(The father's representative starts breathing rapidly and heavily.)*

Payne to Father: What's happening as you say that?

Father: A lot of emotion, but also fear. I feel very, very small, too small. Afraid of him.

Payne: Please say the words again.

Father: Father, please be gentle with me. *(A tear rolls down his face.)*

Payne to Grandfather: How does that feel to hear your son say that?

Grandfather: Nothing. It doesn't touch me at all.

Payne takes a representative to stand in for Sean's great-grandfather. As the great-grandfather stands in place, the grandfather begins to shake.

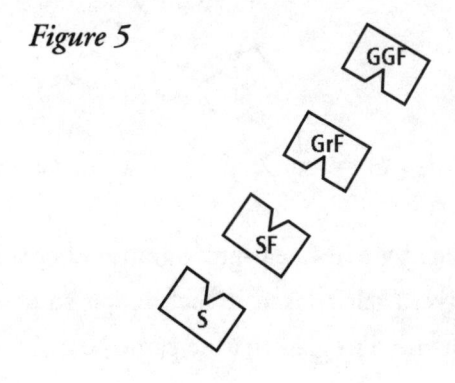

Figure 5

The Language of the Soul

Payne to Grandfather: What is happening here with Grandfather?
Grandfather: I feel afraid.

Payne turns the grandfather around to face his father (Great-grandfather).

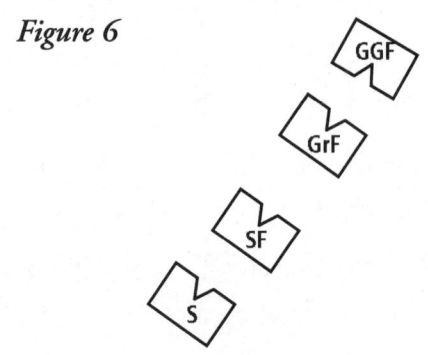

Figure 6

Payne to Grandfather: How does that feel now?
Grandfather: Terrible. I feel so ashamed, like he doesn't want me at all.
Payne to Great-grandfather: How are things here when you look at your son?
Great-grandfather: I feel very strict and harsh. He needs to be a man.

Payne takes a representative to stand in for Sean's great-great-grandfather. As soon as great-great-grandfather is placed, Sean's representative, the father and grandfather all breathe a sigh of relief.

Figure 7

Payne: What happened when Great-great-grandfather stepped in?
Sean's Representative: I felt relaxed. Relief. It was so tense before.
Father: the same for me, I'm glad that he came.

Chapter Two – Expressing the Language of the Soul

Grandfather: I also felt relief, but I'm still a little tense. It's like I'm waiting for something to happen.

Great-grandfather: Nothing much changed for me. I still feel stiff and cold, just a little change, slightly more relaxed, but not much.

Payne to Great-great-grandfather: How are things here?

Great-great-grandfather: I feel great. It's good to see all the men that came after me, my sons.

Payne to Great-great-grandfather: Please say to your son (Great-grandfather), "Fathers are gentle with their sons".

Great-great-grandfather: "Father's are gentle with their sons".

Payne: How does it feel when you say that?

Great-great-grandfather: A little silly, of course I am gentle with my son.

Payne to Great-grandfather: How was it for you to hear that?

Great-grandfather: Strange. Very strange. It's like it is totally new for me. I almost don't understand what he is saying.

Payne to Sean, the client: Did anything special happen with Great-Grandfather?

Sean: As far as I know, he was in the First World War. He was sent to France.

Payne takes a representative to symbolise WWI and places it next to Great-grandfather *and* Great-great-grandfather.

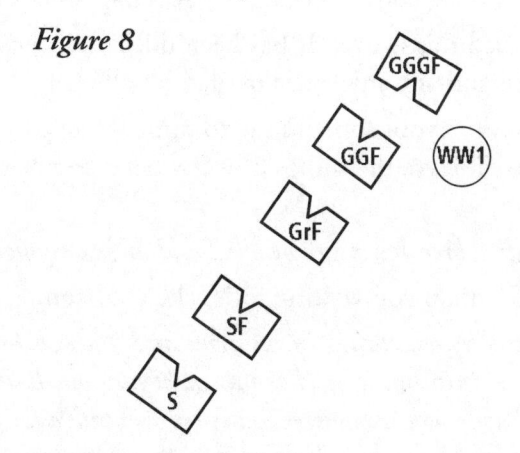

Figure 8

Payne to Great-grandfather: How is that when WWI stands here?

Great-grandfather: It's terrible. I'm all stiff and I can hardly breathe. I can't look at it.

Payne to Great-grandfather: Look at your father and say to him, "Some terrible things happened in this war and I needed you".

Great-grandfather could not utter the words and instead fell into his father's arms and sobbed. After a minute or two, I asked Great-great-grandfather to gently turn his son around so that he could see his own son. Great-great-grandfather whispered into his son's ear, "Look, you have a son", at which point Great-grandfather embraced his son (Grandfather). After a few more moments, Great-grandfather turned his son (Grandfather) around to look at his son (Sean's Father) and whispered in his ear, "Look, you have a son". The men smiled at one another.

Payne to Father: Please say to your father, "Father, please be gentle with me".

Father: Father, please be gentle with me.

Payne to Father: How does it feel to say that?

Father: It feels wonderful. It is like an empty space inside me has been filled.

Grandfather now embraces his son (Father).

Payne to Father: Now it is time for you to look at your son. Let's turn you around. How does that feel when you look at him?

Father: I feel a little guilty, but also relieved, and also happy to see him.

Payne to Mother: I notice you are crying, what is happening with you?

Mother: I'm so relieved this is over. It has been difficult to be here, torn between my husband and my son. I'm glad it's all over.

Payne to Father: Look at your son and say to him, "Beloved son, it is good to see you and we'll leave the things of war where they belong, with my grandfather".

Sean's representative breathes a sigh of relief and looks longingly at his father.

Payne to Father: What are you waiting for? Take your son.

Father takes Sean's representative in his arms and squeezes him tight. Sean's representative relaxes into it and says, "I've missed him so much, it is like I want to climb into him". Payne now exchanges Sean's representative for the client Sean and the two men embrace. Sean breathes very rapidly and deeply, letting out a lot of emotion with his breath.

Payne to Sean: Please look up at your father and say to him, "Father, please be gentle with me".

Sean: Father, please be gentle with me.

Payne: How does that feel, Sean?

Sean: It's great. I'm still a little afraid. I don't know if this can be true or not.

Payne: Just let the constellation work for you and take this image into your Soul. From there, external things will change over time. Now please turn around, leaning slightly up against your father and look at Gavin, who's been waiting here patiently for quite some time.

Payne: How does that feel, Sean?

Sean: Wow. Totally different. I don't feel inferior to him any longer. Actually, I want to introduce him to my father.

Sean crosses the workshop floor and takes Gavin by the hand and they both stand in front of Sean's father.

Payne to Father: How is this for you when your gay son stands here with his partner?

Father: I'm getting used to it. It's OK, no, it's more than OK. It feels good to see my son happy.

Payne to Gavin: How are things for you?

Gavin: It's like a whole weight has lifted off my shoulders. I'm very happy for Sean and I'm happy for myself, too.

Payne to Sean: And how does it feel for you?

Sean: This is so new. Something has changed inside me. I feel taller, like I belong to both of them, to Gavin and to my father. It's like I've "come home".

Payne: Take this inner strength home with you to Gavin. He will notice a difference. It is better that you say nothing or very, very little about what happened here. Just allow this new sense of belongingness to sit with you and allow it to unfold.

The constellation ends.

Conclusion

One of the major keys to healing this trans-generational rift between fathers and their sons was the use of the healing sentence, "Father, please be gentle with me". This expression is a direct appeal from the Soul for love to be restored. As the son speaks these words, he feels his deep longing for his father and his defences begin to fade. Likewise, as the father hears these words, he becomes more aware of the fact that he has a son standing in front of him and, more often than not, he begins to soften.

As we are engaging *the field* in Family Constellation work, we are able to work directly with individuals who have already passed away. In that way, we give the dead a voice. Additionally, we are working directly with the collective emotional body of the family Soul, and, in this case, of the male line. The key to healing this male line was to represent the First World War, an event that had clearly traumatized Sean's great-grandfather. When men return from wars, they are more often than not deeply traumatized and have taught themselves not to feel as a result of losing comrades and seeing terrible things happen to them. Perhaps they are even haunted by the guilt of killing an enemy soldier at close quarters. This numbness, which is designed as a protection mechanism, then plays a part in his relationship with his own children; therefore the feeling is passed on from one generation to the next. The question is, would Sean's experience have been any different if he was not gay? The likelihood is that it may have been very similar; however, the added pressure from the male line of "what a man should be", made it even more challenging for Sean and his father. Many men have difficulty in feeling their children when their own fathers and grandfathers have been to war, as they have learnt the defence mechanism of not feeling.

A few thoughts on support for a gay couple

Although the above constellation found resolution through healing the transgenerational impact of war, it is not to say that all fathers that have difficulty with their gay sons have the same dynamic in their family. Wars, and the possible strictness of religion from previous generations, do indeed have strong influence on the male line, but there can be a myriad of reasons for difficulties.

One of the great difficulties for gay couples is that, in many cases, the relationship is simply not supported by the parents. The vast majority of gay men and women have at one time been rejected outright by one or both parents, or have been rejected in smaller ways, such as, the partner's not being acknowledged as a member of the extended family. In addition, compared to most heterosexual couplings, there are no formal celebrations that create landmarks in the life of the relationship (marriage, wedding anniversaries, the birth of children, christenings etc.). Many gay people move into their adult lives attending the weddings of friends, their friends' children's birthdays, bar and bah mitzvahs, christenings, etc, yet, for the most part, there is little to no reciprocation. Although this also applies to childless heterosexual couples, the added strain of lack of support from the parents takes its toll. It is true that many gay relationships don't last, but how can they if the couple is made up of two individuals who feel that they don't belong? When two individuals don't belong to their families, it is difficult for them to find a sense of belongingness with one another. In the case of Sean and Gavin, Gavin did feel that he belonged, and there was an imbalance in the relationship as he felt he had to compensate for Sean's lack of belonging.

Gay marriages – a legal step forward

In very recent years, the Netherlands, Canada, Spain, Belgium and the United Kingdom have legalized same-sex marriages and civil partnerships, with South Africa due to follow suit in 2006 after a Constitutional Court ruling in 2005.

In my opinion, this is the only way forward. As previously stated, the majority of gay and lesbian individuals have been rejected to some degree by one or both parents, which often leaves a gay couple feeling that there is no support for their relationship. If high and constitutional courts around the world begin to legally acknowledge and honour same-sex relationships, it is my feeling that the entire landscape of same-sex partnerships will change. In decades gone by, nations needed to introduce laws to bring an end to racism. As laws change, we see cultures changing over time and become more accepting of racial diversity. It is not to say that laws eradicate all racism, but they represent a significant cultural change. So it will be for same-sex couples. As governments acknowledge and cease excluding their gay populations, so too will large sections of the population, which in turn will bring respite to the often heavy burden of being gay in today's world.

The *language of the Soul*, which is an expression of the Soul, includes all that there is. If we are to build a soul-led culture and planet, then all citizens and relationships need to be included. We have seen many exclusions down through the ages. African–Americans, Native Americans, Jews in Nazi Germany, victims, perpetrators, unwed mothers, "illegitimate children", and countless other individuals and groups. Many families and nations are living with the consequences of such exclusions.

It has always struck me as significant that the grip of AIDS has been most prominent in those very sections of our world that are excluded – among Africans, gay men, prostitutes and intravenous drug users. These hitherto excluded groups are now having an impact on economies and on the future of growing and developing nations, plus placing burdens on industrialised nations' healthcare systems. As a species, do we need to create such suffering, pain and anguish just to notice those who have been excluded? Just as the individual and family Soul includes that which has been excluded, so too, does the Soul of humanity.

David
"I had an affair"

Payne: What would you like to work with?

David: I've been married for eight years and I've recently had an affair and I don't know what to do about it.

Payne: Is the affair over?

David: Yes, I ended it. It lasted for about three months.

Payne: Did you love this other woman? Do you love your wife?

David: No, I love my wife, not the other woman.

Payne: So what would you like to work with?

David: I don't know how to tell my wife. I am looking for help with that.

Payne: Why do you want to tell her?

David: I feel so guilty and I feel that she has a right to know.

Payne: My dear friend, you're looking for a way to lessen your feelings of guilt. When you tell your wife, you are simply asking her to forgive you. That's not her job, that's your job. You must forgive yourself. My advice is that you say nothing to her. In that way, you will fully own what you have done and carry it in your own Soul instead of trying to share the burden.

David: I didn't expect you to tell me not to tell her.

Payne: And judging by the gasps and faces around the room, no one else expected me to give that answer. I am assuming, of course, that the other woman is not pregnant with your child?

David: No, she isn't.

Chapter Two – Expressing the Language of the Soul

Payne: Why do you feel that you turned away from your wife in that way?

David: We have three children, we're always busy and she is always tired. She's no longer interested in sexual relations, or at least it happens rarely. My affair was purely sexual.

Payne: Has anything special happened in the marriage? Have you lost a child?

David: No, each of our three children is healthy. We did have difficulty in conceiving, though.

Payne: Please explain, what happened?

David: Our first two pregnancies were miscarried. *(David suddenly breaks down and sobs.)* Then we had two children, then another three miscarriages, and then our last child. We always wanted three children. Both my wife and I are only children and we wanted a house full of children so that none of them would be lonely. It's been so difficult.

Payne asks a participant in the workshop to sit next to David, in order to represent his wife.

Payne: Please take her hand, I want to bring something to light for you.

Payne asks five members of the workshop to stand in front of David.

Payne: Do you know who is standing there?

Dave: No, I'm not sure. But I feel something moving inside me.

Payne: These are the miscarried children, all five of them.

David sobs deeply as he looks at the children, his wife's representative also sobs and the two clench their hands together.

Payne: Now look at your wife and say to her, "It was too much and I looked away from you".

David: It was too much and I looked away from you.

Payne: How does that feel?

David: So true, the affair gave me an escape from the heaviness of all of this.

Payne to Wife's Representative: How is this for you?

Wife's Representative: Heavy, very heavy and I want to say the same to him.

Payne: Please, go ahead.

Wife: It was too much and I looked away from you.

The constellation ends.

Payne: This is your fate, David, the fate of your marriage. All you need do is go home and love your wife. Please don't burden her more than she has been burdened already. Your focus now is to embrace the loss together. Perhaps one day your wife may join you here and we can work on these losses together. We could do some further investigating into your respective family systems, but we've done enough for now. Are you clearer?

David: Yes, very clear. I didn't get what I expected, but this is so very clear to me.

Conclusion

When David first explained his reasons for having an extra-marital affair, he did so by explaining that they were both too busy and that his wife was always tired from looking after three children, so she had turned away from him sexually. However, is that really true? What is clear from this constellation is that both individuals have turned away from one another. The healing sentence, "It was too much and I looked away from you", brought that into focus. The example of this constellation is not given to suggest that extra-marital affairs are as a result of miscarriages, but to illustrate once more that the reasons given to explain the symptoms do not touch at the heart of the matter.

Many in the workshop were quite surprised when I advised David not to tell his wife of his affair, some a little outraged. A few individuals felt that I was giving David permission to continue having secret affairs. However, that was clearly not the case. David was looking for help and what he received was deep insight into the reasons why he had the affair. From that point, the couple could begin to heal. David reported feeling guilty about his affair for he was clearly still in love with his wife. So we need to ask ourselves, when we feel guilty for having an affair, what are we really doing when we tell our partner? Are we not seeking to lessen our guilt in some way, in the hope that the other may forgive us and absolve us of our "sin", so to speak? Indeed, that is what we are doing. Therefore, all we are doing is hurting the other person twice. We have already taken trust out of the relationship and now we are asking them to give us something in return. There is great imbalance in that.

Chapter Two – Expressing the Language of the Soul

There is great dignity in owning and carrying our own guilt. Within Family Constellations, we always see a perceptible change in the body language of someone who chooses to carry their own guilt and to own it fully. Far from looking forlorn and weakened by it, as some may expect, quite the opposite is true. Why is that? The Soul is truth itself, and when we live in truth with ourselves and with our Souls, more of our Soul is present, and we become strengthened by that.

Chapter Three

RETRIEVING THE LOST SOUL

Over the years, I've worked with a number of individuals who appear to have lost their Souls. They often have a tell-tale look in their eyes that expresses a deeper searching for that which was lost. In general I have found this to be common amongst individuals who fall into the following categories:

- Descendants of the Holocaust
- Adoptees
- Incubator babies
- Those who have lost a sibling at an early age
- Those who have lost a twin
- Those who have experienced a murder in the family

Lauren
"I feel lost and empty"

Payne: What would you like to work with?

Lauren: I feel lost and empty. I'm constantly searching for some meaning, but there is an emptiness inside of me.

Payne: Did anything particular happen in your family? Early deaths? Tragic accidents? Missing people?

Lauren: No, nothing. And as I know this system quite well, I did ask all of these questions myself, but there is nothing I know of.

Payne: OK, well, we can always investigate and see what a constellation will reveal. Centre yourself and select two people, one for yourself and one to represent the feeling of "I Feel Lost and Empty".

Lauren looks around the room and, according to her feeling, selects representatives for herself and the feeling, "I feel lost and empty". She places them in a standing position within the workshop floor space.

The Language of the Soul

IFL: I feel lost and empty   L: Lauren's representative   M: Mother   F: Father

Figure 1

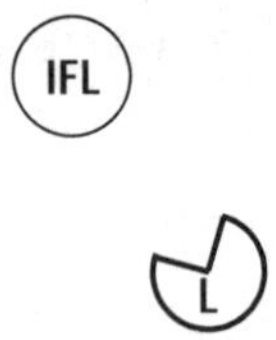

Almost immediately, as the representative for "I Feel Lost and Empty" is placed, this representative starts breathing in a very laboured fashion. We simply sat and observed for a minute or two. As the representative's breathing developed, it began to sound decidedly mechanical, as if it were a machine, not a person.

Payne: This sounds like a breathing apparatus. Were you in an incubator as a child?

Lauren: Yes. I was a premature baby and had some difficulties. I spent six weeks in an incubator.

Payne: Now we have the answer to your feeling. Some therapists refer to this dynamic as an interrupted reaching-out movement. In other words, you could not feel your mother.

Lauren: My mother was very sick and she did not see me for two or three days after I was born. I'm not sure if my father came to see me.

Payne: As you are in your fifties, I can imagine that in those days the men were not allowed much access either to the birth or to you in the incubator. That is an assumption on my part, of course. Thankfully, modern medicine is beginning to change its approach to such trauma. Let us look further.

Payne to Lauren's Representative: How are things for you?

Lauren's Representative: I feel totally frozen, unable to move. I cannot look at this *(pointing to the representative with the laboured breathing)*.

Payne to "I Feel Lost and Empty": How are things here?

"I Feel Lost and Empty": I can hardly breathe. I feel mechanical. I'm not sure I can handle this role for much longer.

Payne: Just relax and simply report what you are feeling instead of allowing it to take you over.

Payne takes a representative for Lauren's mother and places her in the constellation. The mother breaks down immediately on being placed and begins to shake.

Chapter Three – Retrieving the Lost Soul

Figure 2

Payne to Mother: What is happening here?

Mother: It's terrible. I'm shaking all over and I feel desperate.

Payne to Lauren: This was clearly a trauma for your mother, too. How are you doing?

Lauren: I'm trembling inside. This feels very deep. I had no idea how significant it could be.

Payne: Let's bring in your father.

Payne places Father to the right of the mother.

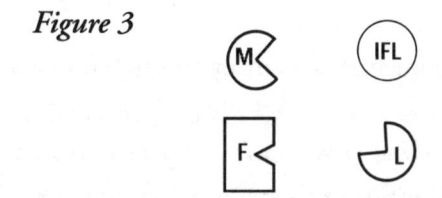

Figure 3

Payne to Mother: Does that make a difference with your husband next to you?

Mother: No, no difference at all. It is as if he is not here.

Payne to Father: And for you? How is it?

Father: I feel nothing.

Payne to Lauren: This is a fairly common reaction for fathers in this position. In previous generations they were totally excluded by the medical profession from birth and such incidents. Additionally, it is a way that many men deal with trauma – they simply close off their feelings and become numb. Generations of wars have taught men how to do this; it is a protection mechanism.

Payne selects a representative for Lauren's maternal grandmother and places her behind Lauren's mother for support.

Payne to Mother: How does that feel now, with your own mother standing behind you?

Mother: It is such a relief, I feel much better and I have the strength to look at this now.

Payne: Please look at your daughter; look her directly in the eyes.

Lauren's representative cries and shakes as her mother looks at her.

Payne: Slowly reach out your hand towards your daughter and feel the support of your own mother behind you. Just allow your hand to stretch out in her direction.

Payne moves to stand next to the daughter, gently placing a hand on her lower back[1].

Payne to Lauren's Representative: Gently allow your own hand to reach out towards your mother, and just breathe through these emotions you are feeling.

As the two women reached towards one another very slowly, the representative for the feeling "I Feel Lost and Empty" begins to breath in a more usual and calm manner.

Payne: Now allow your hands to meet and touch one another.

As their hands meet, the mother suddenly moves forward and embraces her daughter; both are sobbing loudly. It is a very moving scene.

Payne to Lauren's Representative: Now that you are with your mother, look at that part of you that is still stuck in the incubator, the one representing "I Feel Lost and Empty".

Mother and daughter reach out towards "I Feel Lost and Empty", and this representative "falls" into them and they hold her up, gently caressing her. Eventually, all three women feel well and Father smiles.

---

[1] The lower back is the area of the sacrum. During trauma, a child will separate itself from the lower half of its body energetically. The sacrum and the coccyx areas of the body house energy vortexes known as chakras. The first chakra is situated near the coccyx and it holds our will to live and the quality and quantity of vibrant physical energy. The second chakra, located in the area of the sacrum, holds our ability to give and receive physical and sexual pleasure. When a baby experiences a trauma, these two centres either become damaged or do not develop fully, thus limiting our ability to stand fully in life and to feel others. During a constellation dealing with such trauma, I place my hand gently at the base of the spine or on the area of the sacrum in order to encourage increased energy flow as the trauma is being released. For further work on releasing traumas held in this area, I recommend Qi-Gong as a regular practice, and energy work conducted by graduates of the Barbara Brennan School of Healing or the Snow Lion Center School.

Lauren's representative is replaced with the client Lauren. She also "falls" into her mother and a deep sob is voiced. They are both left with this movement for a couple of minutes.

Payne to Lauren: Lay your head on its side on your mother's chest and open your mouth towards her heart. Imagine that you are breathing in her heart, in other words, her love. Just keep your mouth open and breathe deeply.

Payne stands behind Lauren and places his hand on her lower back, encouraging her to breathe in her mother.

After a few more minutes, Lauren returns to the chair next to Payne.

Payne: How do you feel now?

Lauren: Different.

Payne: In which way?

Lauren: I'm not really sure. I feel more clear, my eyes are more open. More alive…but it's a totally new feeling.

Payne: Allow this constellation to work for you. You've just been through a very deep process, so give it time to work for you. It may feel as if you have just woken up from a deep sleep and that you need time to orientate yourself in the new environment that you find yourself in.

Lauren: That's it exactly, it feels as if I've just got out of bed, but there's a new clarity there as I'm starting to wake up. Thank you.

Conclusion

Such traumas are not only caused by birth trauma or time in an incubator, but it can also be caused by a child spending time in hospital a little later on in life. (It would seem that the younger the child, the deeper the trauma.) In years gone by, often parents and children were kept apart during the child's time in hospital, perhaps only allowed to visit for an hour or two per day. As we are becoming more aware of the impact of childhood trauma, hospitals are increasingly accommodating towards parents and encouraging their presence, even to the extent of allowing mothers to sleep overnight next to their child. However, not all such traumas are avoidable, especially when the mother herself is sick, or her own life has been in danger. As was clear with Lauren's constellation, her mother was also deeply traumatized by this event and her father had simply suppressed all feelings on the matter.

The benefit of such constellation work is that it not only releases personal trauma, but also begins the process of releasing trauma from the family Soul, or collective "field" of experience. Our mother is our first experience of intimacy, she nourishes us within her body and we have a sense of being "one" with her. Once we are born, she touches us and breastfeeds us, all of which lays the foundation for future intimate relationships with other human beings. When this connection to mother is severed by birth traumas, it dictates in our adult life how we relate to others and our sense of being and belonging.

Christine
"I feel alone and directionless"

Payne: What would you like to work with?

Christine: I feel lonely and directionless. I've walked out of a good marriage, walked out of friendships. It feels as if I've never been able to find what I'm looking for and I'm not even sure what I am looking for.

Payne: Do you have any children?

Christine: No, and I've never been pregnant, as far as I know.

Payne: Please tell me about your family of origin.

Christine: I'm an only child. My mother had difficulty in conceiving, so my parents were married for some time before I was born. It was her one and only pregnancy.

Payne: Any special circumstances? Did your parents divorce or have other partners or marriages before one another?

Christine: No, they were quite young and are still married to this day.

Payne: Any significant events in their own families of origin? Missing individuals, early deaths?

Christine: No, nothing that I know of. My father was one of four, my mother one of three.

Payne: Well, let's start with the basic family and we'll see what is revealed, shall we?

Christine: Yes, that's OK.

Payne instructs Christine to select representatives for herself, her mother and her father.

Chapter Three – Retrieving the Lost Soul

M: Mother   F: Father   C: Christine   T: Twin   PG: Paternal Grandfather
MG: Maternal Grandmother

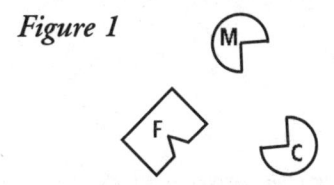

Figure 1

Payne: Your mother looks sad. But let us have a look.

Payne to Mother: How are things here?

Mother: As you said, sad. I have difficulty looking at my daughter standing there.

Payne to Christine's Representative: How are things here?

Christine's Representative: I feel very sad and desperate. I want my mother to look at me. I can't look at my father at all. I feel something beside me, and it makes me very sad.

Payne to Father: How are things with you?

Father: I'm not really here and I find it difficult to look at my daughter.

Payne to Christine's Representative: How does that "something" beside you feel?

Christine's Representative: Frightening, but also deeply sad. It is so palpable.

Payne to Christine the Client: Has anyone died? It would seem that there is someone missing and they all feel it. Did a child die that you know of?

Christine: *(Wiping tears from her eyes)* Not a living child. I was conceived as a twin and my mother had a miscarriage at three months. She thought it was all over but after medical examinations they discovered that she was still pregnant; I had survived.

Payne: This is indeed a difficult fate.

Payne takes a representative for Christine's twin and places her standing to the right of Christine, very close to her.

The Language of the Soul

Figure 2

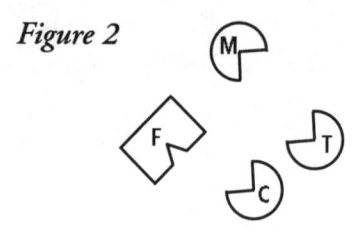

Payne to Christine's Representative: How does that feel when your twin stands next to you?

Christine: Unbearable sadness. I can hardly stand to look at her. I feel guilty. Such deep guilt.

Payne to Mother: How is it for you when your daughter's twin stands there next to her?

Mother: Also unbearable. It is very difficult to look at and I feel very weak. I could almost pass out.

Payne to Father: And how is it for you?

Father: It's like I'm not here. I really don't want to look over there (*at the twins*).

Payne takes two representatives from the workshop audience and places a grandfather behind the father and a grandmother behind the mother for support.

Payne to Father: How does that feel with your father behind you?

Father: Better. I feel a little stronger. I can almost look there now.

Payne to Mother: How does that feel with your mother behind you?

Mother: Better. I am much calmer now.

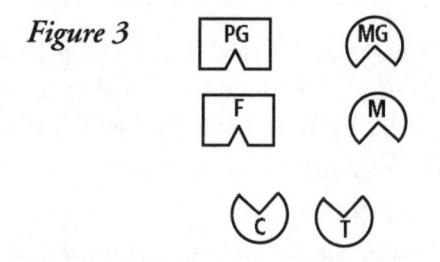

Figure 3

Payne asks Christine's representative to sit down and replaces her in the constellation with Christine the client.

Payne to Christine: Please look at your twin. How does that feel?

Christine: Difficult. I feel as if it should have been me that died, not her.

Payne: Say to her, "It's been very difficult without you, and I've always wondered where you were".

Christine: *(Finding it very difficult to get the words out)* It's been very difficult without you, and I've always wondered where you were.

Christine spontaneously flings her arms around her twin and the two women sob deeply for some minutes.

Payne to Christine: Please say to her, "Please smile upon me kindly if I live".

Christine: Please smile upon me kindly if I live.

Payne: How did it feel to say that?

Christine: Difficult. I feel guilty that she died, very guilty.

Payne to Twin: How do you feel?

Twin: Very glad to see my sister, but otherwise neutral.

Payne to Twin: Please say to your sister, "It was my fate".

Twin: It was my fate.

Payne to Christine: How does that feel now?

Christine: A slight change.

Payne to Christine: Please look at your parents and tell me how that feels.

Christine: Terrible! It feels like they are blaming me for something. I don't want to look at them.

Payne: Let's work more directly with this.

Payne takes the twin and places her gently in front of the parents, instructing her to rest her head on their shoulders. The mother and father embrace their lost child and weep together.

Payne to Mother: Please look your husband in the eyes and say to him, "We mourn together".

Mother: We mourn together.

Payne to Father: Now please say the same thing to your wife.

Father: We mourn together

Payne to Father & Mother: How does that feel now?

Father: I'm feeling it now. I was numb before, and now I can feel both my child and my wife.

Mother: It feels as if a burden has lifted. I had to do it all alone until now.

Payne to Mother and Father: Now look across at your living daughter and say to her, "You are our living child, and it's good to see you".

Mother and Father: You are our living child, and it's good to see you.

Both Mother and Father reach out towards Christine and beckon her to join in their embrace. Christine moves across to them and joins her twin and her parents. After a few moments, the work continues.

Payne to Christine: Please look at your sister and say to her, "It's pity that you couldn't stay, because I've missed you".

Christine: It's a pity that you couldn't stay because I've missed you terribly. *(Christine embraces her sister and sobs deeply.)*

Payne to Christine: Now say to her, "I now take you as my sister and give you a place in my heart".

Christine: I now take you as my sister and give you a place in my heart.

Payne: How does that feel?

Christine: Even though we can't know for sure, it feels really right to say "sister".

Payne: Now say to her, "Please wait for me patiently, I'll come when it's my proper time. Meanwhile I shall live my life fully in honour of you".

Christine: Please wait for me patiently, I'll come when it's my proper time. Meanwhile I shall live my life fully in honour of you.

Payne: How does it feel when you say that?

Christine: It's still sad, but it feels right. It is almost as if I didn't feel that I had the right to be either happy or to live. So saying that I'll live my life in honour of her feels really good, it's a relief. I feel more comfortable with my parents now, too. They can see me, and that's a good feeling.

Note: Recent studies have suggested that up to 82% of pregnancies start as twins and only 7% result in live full-term twin births. It is also estimated that one in every eight children born, started life as a twin and that the other child was either miscarried or "re-absorbed" in the first trimester. This is referred to as "Vanishing Twin Syndrome".

What I have observed through Family Constellation work where we employ the information coming to us from the "field", is that all occupants of the womb are, on one level or another, aware of all other previous occupants. For example, when a couple has suffered a miscarriage, we often see that the representatives for the living children report feeling either relieved or more clear on their place in the world when the miscarried child is represented as one of their siblings – even when the miscarriage took place before their own birth.

Over the past few years, I have witnessed a number of constellations where a representative reports feeling that something is missing, either to their right or left side. In such cases, a representative is asked to take that place and invariably the representative feels "more complete" or relieved. Sometimes, there is also grief. With this kind of constellation, it is difficult to really know if what is being felt is an actual twin, or a child that was miscarried in a previous or later pregnancy. However, at times, the representatives either stand shoulder to shoulder or one rests their head on the other's shoulder and they look as if they are "one". This often looks and feels like a twin and at times a representative will spontaneously say, "This feels like my twin" without any suggestion or encouragement.

A couple of years ago a woman set up a constellation of her family. During the process of her constellation, her representative and one of the representatives for another sibling reported, "It feels like someone is missing". As I placed the extra representative, she stood shoulder-to-shoulder with my client's representative. As I looked, I asked the client, "It is possible that you could be a twin?" In that instant both the client and her representative fainted. A few days later the client called me to say that she had asked her father if it was possible that she was a twin. Her father reported to her that her mother had had a miscarriage in the first trimester, then later discovered that she was still pregnant. The doctor had said that she had probably lost one of a set of twins. My client had had no conscious knowledge of these events until that point.

Conclusion

Christine's parents were clearly grieved by the loss of Christine's twin. I have often observed that when a couple loses a child, it is very difficult for them to see their living children, each child being a reminder of what has been lost. This is often carried deeply by the living children, as they feel unseen. In

Christine's case, there was the bitter-sweet experience of both the loss of a child and the birth of a child from the same pregnancy. In such cases when a twin is lost, it often becomes unbearable for the parents to look at the surviving twin as the reminder of that which has been lost is even more acute. Such responses to the loss of a twin left Christine feeling guilty simply for being alive and she expressed directly, "It should have been me". The challenge for Christine is to find a sense of "I", even though she started life as a "we". Her constellation was the start of a long process of replacing her lonely and directionless feeling as she gave her twin sister a place in her heart and began to feel that she could live her life fully in honour of her sister.

Let us look at the healing sentence, "I shall live my life fully in honour of you". This sentence does not suggest that she will live her dead twin's life for her. On the contrary, it acknowledges that one death is sufficient, and that for her not to live life fully would be to dishonour her twin's death. Through constellation work, the dead in essence are given a voice through the representatives. What we have observed is that in the vast majority of cases, the representatives for the dead feel relieved when the living decide to get on with their lives and live fully. The dead, it would seem, have no wish for anyone to continue the suffering or to hold themselves back from living out of respect for them. To the contrary, they often report feeling either distressed or irritated when another sacrifices their happiness for them. For the most part, the dead are in total acceptance of their fate; it is the living who have a problem with their fate. Through the strong bond of twins, it often appears in constellations that the dead twin is not at rest until their living twin accepts and bows to their fate and chooses to live their life.

Robyn
"Death is all around me"

Payne: What would you like to work with today?

Robyn: Death seems to follow me everywhere. Friends die, colleagues die. People die in accidents and one has even been murdered. It seems as if death is haunting me.

Payne: Were there any deaths in your family?

Robyn: Yes, when I was eleven my eight-year-old brother drowned in the swimming pool.

Payne: Who was present?

Chapter Three – Retrieving the Lost Soul

Robyn: Myself and my elderly grandfather.

Payne: Your parents were not present?

Robyn: No, they were out for the day.

Payne: Well, let's work with this directly. Please select representatives for your grandfather, your mother and father, yourself and your younger brother.

GF: Grandfather   F: Father   M: Mother   B: Brother   R: Robyn

Figure 1

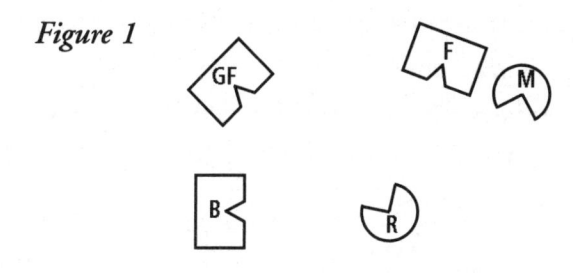

Payne to Grandfather: How are things with you?

Grandfather: I want to sink into the ground. I feel very guilty and I can't look at anyone.

Payne to Robyn's Representative: How are things here?

Robyn's Representative: I want to lie on the floor. I feel terrible.

Payne to Father and Mother: How are things with you?

Mother: I am beyond grief and I can't look at anyone else, only my son, but even that is difficult.

Father: I feel guilty, but also numb in a way. It's an odd feeling. I also cannot look at anyone.

Payne instructs the representatives to follow their feelings through physical movement. The representative for Robyn's brother lays down flat on his back. Robyn's representative curls up on the floor next to him, facing his direction.

Figure 2

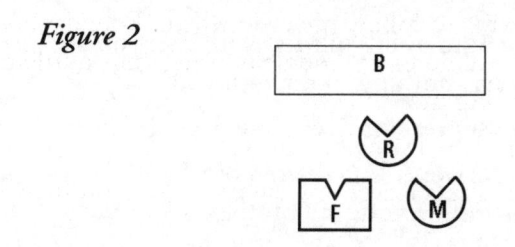

The Language of the Soul

Payne to Robyn's Representative: How are things now?

Robyn's Representative: Peaceful. I want to be with him. I want to die.

Payne instructs the representative for Robyn's brother to speak whatever feelings come up.

Robyn's Brother: It makes me sad to see you here. You're not supposed to be dead.

Payne to Brother: Say to Robyn "My place is with the dead, it was my fate"

Brother: My place is with the dead, it was my fate

Robyn puts her arms around her brother and weeps.

Robyn's Representative: It's very difficult to leave him. It's so peaceful here.

Payne to Robyn's Representative: Please stand up and look at your grandfather and parents.

Payne to Father and Mother: Say to your daughter, "You were just a child, the responsibility lies with us".

Mother and Father: You were just a child, the responsibility lies with us.

Payne Robyn's Representative: How does that feel?

Robyn's Representative: Better. It brings a little relief.

Payne to Grandfather: Please say to your granddaughter, "You were just a child, the responsibility also lies with me".

Grandfather: You were just a child... *(loud sobs)*... the responsibility also lies with me.

Payne to Robyn's Representative: How does that feel?

Robyn's Representative: A little worse, I want to help my grandfather. He looks terrible.

Payne to Grandfather: Please say to your granddaughter, "The burden of guilt lies with me, you are just the grandchild, it has nothing to do with you".

Grandfather: The burden of guilt lies with me, you are just the grandchild, it has nothing to do with you.

Payne to Robyn's Representative: How does that feel now?

Robyn's Representative: A little better, but I still feel the pull to go down to the ground and be with my brother.

Payne replaces Robyn's representative for the client Robyn.

Payne to Robyn: Did you go to your brother's funeral?

Robyn: No. Also, my parents forbade me from ever talking about him. Even to this day, and I'm now 46 years old, I've never spoken to my mother about David, my brother.

Payne: You see, when a child does not attend a funeral, it is difficult for them to believe that the other is really dead. That makes it difficult and life can be filled with the continual feeling of searching for that person. Even for adults, accepting death is difficult.

Allow me to relate a story about my own mother's death in 2004. She died very suddenly and I received a call from my father telling me of her sudden death. The next thing I knew I was on a plane from South Africa back home to Gibraltar. When I arrived, I fully expected to see or hear my mother in the kitchen making something for all of us. I arrived on Sunday and the funeral was on Tuesday. For two days, I kept expecting her to either come down the stairs or magically appear in the kitchen. In my mind, she was ill in hospital. Even on the morning of the funeral, as we were walking towards the funeral home to view her body, I was convinced that we were on our way to the hospital to visit her. Her death did not become real for me until I saw her body in the coffin. Even then, there was a part of me still in denial. The woman in the coffin did not look like my memory of my mother, as I hadn't seen her for a year. It took several weeks before I finally accepted that she was no longer with us. I relate this to you as a forty-four-year-old man, and it happened less than two years ago. You were eleven when your brother died. You did not go to the funeral and you were then forbidden to speak of him. Let's continue with our work.

Payne instructs the representatives for Robyn's parents to stand behind her, her brother lying on the floor in front of them.

Payne to Robyn and Parents: Please kneel beside the grave of your brother and son.

All three kneel in front of David's body.

Payne to Mother: Gently take Robyn's hand and guide it towards David's body until you touch it.

Robyn sobs. As she does so, she is no longer the middle-aged client who came to the workshop, but the eleven-year-old girl who was not allowed to attend her brother's funeral. Her parents, also sobbing, comfort their daughter. The scene is deeply moving. As Robyn stood once more, there was a perceptible change in the look in her eyes, a new fresh sparkle.

The Language of the Soul

Robyn: Although I feel very sad still, I feel released in a way.

Payne: We're not quite done yet.

Payne instructs the representative for David to stand up and look at his sister.

Payne to Robyn: Please look your brother directly in the eyes and say, "It's a great pity that you left so early, for I have missed you dearly".

Robyn: It's a great pity that you left so early, for I have missed you dearly.

Payne: How is that?

Robyn: Still sad, but it is easy to look at him and easy to say.

Payne: Now say to him, "Please bless me if I live my life fully".

Robyn: Please bless me if I live my life fully.

Payne: How does that feel?

Robyn: That's a lot more difficult to say.

Payne: Now say to him, "Only one person died on that day and I dishonour you if I live as if dead".

Robyn: Only one person died on that day and I dishonour you if I live as if dead.

Payne: And now?

Robyn: Phew, I feel as if I am more awake now, like something has lifted.

Payne: Now say to him, "One day we shall be together, please wait for me patiently".

Robyn: One day we shall be together, please wait for me patiently.

Robyn and David smile at each other broadly and embrace.

Payne: How do you feel now?

Robyn: I feel very different, much more alive, somehow, and more accepting of his death.

Payne: The grief regarding the death of your brother will never go away, for it is appropriate to mourn those who are close to us. However, it will become manageable and simply a part of you. What is now different is the guilt concerning the circumstances of his death has been left with those who were the adults at the time. This is not a judgment, it is simply a movement to shift that responsibility away from you, for you were far too young at the age of eleven to be given such a responsibility. Now that you are free of the guilt and have met your brother's death face on, you are free to live life more fully, instead of living as if you yourself are dead.

Robyn called me on the phone about a week after this constellation reporting that she feels much more alive and more willing to actually remain living and to discover more of what life has to offer.

Comment

I have worked with many clients who have lost siblings when they were children or teenagers. It would seem that in some cultures it is very common practice not to allow children to attend funerals, even when the dead person is a very close family member such as a father, brother or sister. Just as I related in my story to Robyn about my own denial regarding my mother's death at the age of 42, for children, when they do not attend a funeral, they are left never really believing that the individual died. From observing many constellations of this nature, I have seen that this often leaves them living life as if dead themselves, or in a sort of "no man's land", somewhere between this world and the next.

Often, when a sibling dies, the living children feel guilty for living, even when the death is related to an illness, rather than an accident as in Robyn's case. From what I've observed, a part of the living siblings also dies, which can lead them to living lives that feel directionless or empty, bereft of the feeling of their own Soul. Through the representation of a funeral scene, the Soul of the client can be retrieved from the grave and life can be led once more.

Another aspect of the guilt such clients feel is that they are often reluctant to live happy and fulfilled lives out of the fear that it somehow disrespects their parents' grief. Through constellation work and the employment of the "field", we more often than not see that the parents cease to see their living children clearly from the moment another child dies. This is deeply felt by the remaining siblings and this contributes to their feeling of guilt for simply being alive. Family Constellation work is a very powerful way of bringing resolution to these feelings in a way that is direct, devoid of stories, and efficient in its outcome. (Many of the clients I have dealt with have spent many years in psychotherapy trying to resolve their conflicting feelings.)

Conclusion

The two crucial healing sentences were:

"Please bless me if I live my life fully"

and

"Only one person died on that day and I dishonour you if I live as if dead".

As Robyn expressed, "Please bless me if I live my life fully", it highlighted her feelings of guilt for simply living. One of the greatest blocks to resolving such issues is our not accepting the fate of others. We often feel that we are being disloyal to the dead if we accept their fate – as if that in itself would be a betrayal of our loved one. However, as the field is employed, not only are the living represented with great accuracy, but so indeed are the dead. Although this is an assumption, if we are able to witness the often pinpoint accuracy of a constellation and how the living are represented, it is very safe to assume that this accuracy is a global truth that also applies to the representation of the dead. Almost without exception, the dead are peaceful, accepting of their fate, and they feel great relief when the living get on with their lives. At times I have witnessed slight annoyance or a feeling of dismay when a living person sabotages their own life out of loyalty to the dead. At times, however, I have witnessed "the dead" who are restless and not entirely comfortable with their own fate. This is more often than not related to a person who either died unlawfully or died as a result of cruelty or an injustice. Quite often in Family Constellation work we cross the bridge from psychotherapeutic process into the realm of spiritual healing, where the Souls of those who have not accepted their fate are assisted in moving towards their ancestors or going "into the light". Some examples of that will follow.

During Robyn's constellation, she reported that the representative even "felt" like her brother. As the "field" is engaged, indeed the energies of all who are represented become present, at times to the extent that others report that they can even smell their mother, grandfather, brother, etc. As the experience of David actually being present became strong for Robyn, the healing sentence, "Only one person died on that day and I dishonour you if I live as if dead", brought an awareness to Robyn. With this new awareness, she was totally able to understand that indeed only one person had died and that it was a disservice to her brother to live as if dead.

There is another aspect of this dynamic that affects the living children when a sibling dies. The surviving children perceive that the parents are only able to see their dead sibling and are no longer able to look at them. Hence, there appears to be an impulse to live as if dead in order to fall within the parents' scope of vision. This is often coupled with a deep-seated belief that they do not have their parents' permission to leave. Often, when a boy dies, the daughters may also have feelings of guilt towards their father, even feeling that it would have been better for them to have died so that the father would have been left with a son. In a largely patriarchal society, such feelings are not a surprise.

Entities

When I use the word "entities" in my workshop, it very often conjures up an image in the minds of some participants of "ghosts" or "evil spirits" and notions of "possession". From the many constellations I have facilitated where there appears to be a grave disturbance in the field, and from the work I have done with Brennan Healing Science practitioners, I have come to a greater understanding of what is taking place in terms of entities and their nature.

In addition to our physical body, we also have an energy body that is made up of three parts: emotional body, mental body and spiritual body. At death, the spiritual body separates from the physical body, taking with it the consciousness of the Soul to a level of vibration that is separate from the physical world – in other words, to another reality or dimension. As this happens, the emotional body is cast off and dissipates. However, it has been observed that when a death is caused by great trauma, cruelty, torture or another injustice, the emotional body can retain some cohesion and can continue to exist with its own sense of self. Multiple Personality Disorder, or, more correctly, Dissociative Identity Disorder, in living humans can be employed after an extreme trauma occurs, as a defense mechanism against stressors in the environment. The individual experiences their psyche/identity as disconnected, or split into distinct parts. It would seem evident then, that when death is caused by an extreme trauma, part of an individual can split off and remain as an entity in its own right within the family system.

What has been observed within family systems is that the universal principle of "that which is excluded will be represented (included)" holds true on all levels. Just as a daughter or son may be identified with father's first fiancée within the system, so it is also true that individuals can be entangled with the fate of an ancestor who was murdered, even several generations later.

When this occurs, the entity that remains as a result of a cruel or very traumatic death can appear to be attached to the client. In some cases, the client may even feel that they are living someone else's life and not their own.

In previous generations, individuals with schizophrenia and other mental ailments were often considered to be possessed by demons or by troubled spirits. However, having worked with a number of both schizophrenic clients and those with bi-polar disorder, it would appear that in the majority of cases a "trauma entity" is in some way associated with them. More often than not, these attachments only take place when the murder, cruelty or injustice is either unacknowledged or kept as a secret. In such cases, both the perpetrator and the victim become excluded when the crime is hidden. As the family Soul seeks to include that which has been excluded, an individual may be identified with the victim and/or the perpetrator, and therefore carry the feelings of one or both individuals. As a side note, it is also important to mention that I have worked with individuals who feel that they have experienced sexual abuse as a young child. However, constellations at times reveal that the abuse took place a generation or two back. What this reveals is that the client is in some way identified with the hidden abuse and consequently carries all of the feelings. This is more common when the true victim is either the client's mother, grandmother or great-grandmother.

When working with entities, the client is usually unaware of the actual events that have taken place in previous generations. At most, they may be aware of some rumour or vague story about a great-grandparent or some other distant relative. However, the events may have taken place many generations earlier, even ten to fifteen generations earlier or more, and therefore we rely solely on the "field" to inform us through the feelings and actions of the representatives in the constellation. When such events reveal themselves through a constellation, the energy is very palpable and at times even odors such as "death" and "feces" can become present in the workshop space. In such cases, it is important that the facilitator remain centered and unintimidated.

At times, working with a trauma entity can be very stressful for the client in question. However, for the most part, clients not only feel relieved and much better after resolution is found, but also look physically different. These physical differences can manifest in a younger, more healthful-looking face, or in a general change in posture, now that the drain on their energy resources has been healed.

Chapter Three – Retrieving the Lost Soul

When we consider history, we must take into consideration the transgenerational impact of atrocities and cruelty in times gone by and consider the possibility that many of us may have ancestors whose "spirits" are not yet at rest, thus creating an energy drain on the family Soul as opposed to being a source of positive support. So what of the descendents of the African slaves? Or those whose ancestors were lynched, burnt at the stake or forced to flee a land, leaving their children behind? Many events have left their indelible mark on the Soul of humanity: Pogroms, the Holocaust, the persecution of Huguenots, enslaving of Africans, witch hunts and burnings, ethnic "cleansing", the horrors of the Conquistadors in South America, just to name a few. Additionally, in some cultures across the globe, many baby girls have been murdered or simply left to die in response to a cultural demand for boys. In some eastern and central European countries, some women have had up to ten abortions or more, all of which can contribute to a feeling of "haunting" or a "curse" on later generations. In previous generations, when contraception was either not readily available to the poor or non-existent, it would appear that many children were simply left to die by their exhausted mothers who could not face raising yet another child. As much as we in this modern age can have great sympathy for our great-grandmothers who may have done this, through constellations and the revelations of the field it would appear that, no matter how sympathetic we may be to their plight, such events do still leave a residual impact for the following generations. Let us now look at some examples.

Loretta
"There's a curse on my family"

Payne to Loretta: What would you like to work with today?

Loretta: I have two concerns. The main one is that my daughter does not speak to me, and the second is that I've felt for a long time that there is a curse that follows me around. Even psychics have said there is something evil hanging around me.

Payne: Whilst some psychics with integrity can assist us in seeing that which we are blind to, or assist us in making better choices, I would advise you not to buy into such fearful stories. These stories can do much more harm than good. Let's say that what the psychic told you is true. Did she offer you a solution or simply give you the information?

Loretta: No, she simply gave me the information. She even told me not to speak to my daughter and to accept that as part of my fate with this curse that is upon me.

Payne: Well, let's start with a simple constellation. Select a representative for your daughter and yourself.

Loretta selects a representative for both herself and her daughter and places them facing one another. A few seconds after the placement, her daughter's representative runs to the other side of the room, clutches a wall and begins to shake, as with terror.

Payne to Daughter's Representative: What is happening here?

Daughter's Representative: I'm terrified of her. I want to get as far away as possible.

Payne to Loretta's Representative: How are things here?

Loretta's Representative: I'm also scared. I feel nauseous and there's a feeling of heaviness behind me.

Payne to Loretta: Please tell me about your parents. Where were they from?

Loretta: Italy.

Payne: Why did they leave?

Loretta: For a better life. My father left as a child. He never spoke of Italy, unlike my mother.

Payne takes a representative for Loretta's father and places him in the constellation. The instant that he steps into the field, he covers his head and face with his arms and begins shaking.

Payne to Loretta: There seems to be something here. Tell me more about your father's family. Were they involved in any war or political problems? Were there any deaths that you know of?

Loretta: No, nothing. I don't know. My father never spoke about Italy or his family. He never wanted to.

Payne to Loretta: Well, let's look further.

Payne takes a representative for Loretta's grandfather and places him in the constellation.

Chapter Three – Retrieving the Lost Soul

D: Daughter   GF: Grandfather   F: Father   M: Mother (Loretta)

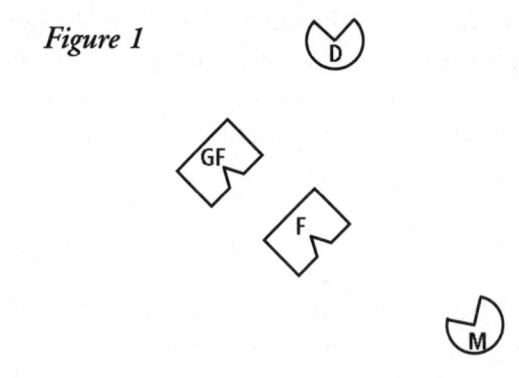

Figure 1

As Grandfather was placed in the constellation, he immediately fell to the ground and, like Loretta's father (his son), he covered his head and face with his arms. However, there was a distinct difference. This representative looked mentally ill and also crawled, made noises and appeared deeply traumatized.

Payne to Daughter's Representative: How are things now? A little better for me because the focus is now over there (pointing to her grandfather and great-grandfather), but it's still terrible and frightening. I still feel sick.

Payne to Loretta's Representative: And how are things for you?

Loretta's Representative: I feel paralyzed with fear and also nauseous.

Payne to Loretta the Client: Do you have any idea at all what this might be? Any stories? Rumours of any kind about your father's family?

Loretta: I'm trying to think, but nothing. As I said, my father never spoke about Italy.

Payne: What is clear is that something terrible happened.

Payne takes a representative for an unknown benevolent ancestor who could have a beneficial influence on the constellation. However, despite the kindly presence of this ancestor, there was no change to the writhing trauma that was unfolding within the constellation. As a next step, he then takes an un-named representative for "the light". In such cases it is better not to tell this representative who or what they are representing in order to avoid any interpretations of "the light" or "god". This type of "blind" representation preserves the authenticity of the representation.

As the presence of "the light" was felt, the constellation calmed down and the energies in the room became serene. The high levels of anxiety felt by the mother and daughter subsided and the next movement in the constellation ended with Loretta's grandfather being embraced by "the light". Immediately afterwards, the representative for Loretta's daughter joined in the embrace with the light and her great-grandfather and Loretta herself stepped into the constellation as her representative gracefully departed. The conclusion was one of great love, gentleness and affection.

The light

When "the light" is placed in a constellation, it is non-specific and does not have any particular religious connotation. However, as "the light" does have religious, spiritual and healing meaning for humanity, it is expressed as a neutral presence of healing within a constellation. The participants are free to draw their own meaning from such a presence. Owing to both the religious and spiritual associations with "the light", I always select a representative for the light without informing them in advance. In this way, we avoid unnecessary interpretation of such a presence and allow the representative to be as authentic as possible. Each and every representative I have ever used as "the light" has reported that it was a wonderful, peaceful encounter with a sense of neutrality combined with compassion that they have never previously experienced. In this role, individuals are able to experience the difference between being truly neutral and being indifferent. In this way, they are able to represent a healing force that others may employ without the need to interfere in the process.

Conclusion

With constellations in which the facts are not known, I have always found it better to encourage the client to leave the story exactly where it is, within the constellation, and not to go searching for evidence of its authenticity. Often there are deep secrets surrounding such events and, for the most part, the best approach is simply to submit to the secret and leave it where it is. At times the energy of sexual abuse can show up in a constellation concerning one generation when the actual events belong to an earlier generation. In such cases as Loretta's, it is difficult to know exactly where the trauma belongs, but it is clear that various members within her family system, including herself and her daughter, have been deeply affected by it.

In the break after this constellation concluded, one of the representatives reported seeing an image of himself in a deep well looking up towards the opening. What are we to conclude about such images and feelings? Is it of any benefit to the client if they are analyzed? In my experience, the answer is no. Once a resolution has been found and the constellation has had a healing effect, the stories of the representatives would only serve to dilute the constellation and the work we have done. In this case, it would be foolhardy to conclude that an individual had been thrown into a well and met their physical demise under such circumstances. As it appeared that we were dealing with a trauma entity, a representative for "the light" was placed in the constellation in order to assist this entity to move on into the light. The image of looking up a well shaft towards the light is a common one reported in near-death experiences. Was the image experienced by the representative information from the "field" about the victim's death, or was it an experience of the entity's journey through the tunnel towards the light? We will never know. The only thing that is important is the healing resolution and the effect it has on the client in question.

It is often very tempting for us to search for intellectual satisfaction; we simply want to know what happened. However, as we cross over into the domain of the Soul and the non-physical influences on our lives, we often can't know, and it would seem to me that it is better simply left that way, with a sense of deep respect for the mystery.

The trauma entity

So far we have explored the presence of entities that arise out of a traumatic and generally unjust death somewhere within the extended family system. At times, however, it would appear that some individuals are influenced by an entity that has been created by their own consciousness. An individual may report having defined goals, a zest for life, and a will to create loving relationships, successful careers and better health in their lives yet many things simply do not come to fruition. They may also have a sense of sabotaging themselves. Although these symptoms are very often true for individuals who have lost siblings or a parent at an early age, and often for women who have had abortions, it is also true for those who have experienced an early childhood trauma, such as time in an incubator or hospitalisation as a very young child.

Just like the symbolism contained within the fairy tale, Snow White and the Seven Dwarfs, each of us has different aspects of ourselves that can be called sub-personalities. There is a part of us that is the pessimist; another that is the hero or heroine; the priest; the pauper; the prostitute; the gallant, noble and generous part of ourselves – all of which have been born out of childhood experience and our interpretation of the world. In the case of trauma, however, a sub-personality can assume a far more influential role. Having said this, I am not referring to Dissociative Personality Disorder, but rather to a part of ourselves that serves to protect us from any future harm. This kind of sub-personality does not manifest itself as a different personality but simply runs in the background, having a great deal of influence on our life's choices, responses and reactions, or emerging in times of stress or crisis. For the trauma entity, stress and crisis may not be what we traditionally view as such things but can be triggered by success and the offer of love.

Our lives are filled with problems and challenges, both real and imagined. For the most part they are imagined, and many problems are imagined into existence until they become real and definable. The trauma entity holds onto the memory of a childhood event and imagines that, at every turn, it could happen again. Therefore, it sees its job to be a protector that will take us out of harm's way and circumnavigate events that could recur. In essence, the trauma entity is motivated by fear and it misguidedly seeks to protect us through its own version of love. Owing to its actions and often hidden belief systems, although we may have a conscious desire for something that will bring more joy into our lives, the entity's influence often steers us away from our stated goals and desires. In this book and in my previous book, *The Healing of Individuals, Families and Nations,* we explore and reveal how hidden loyalties to those who have suffered can and do influence our well-being on many levels. In this section, we are exploring how our own direct experience of the world as children also plays a part.

Jane

"I'm not good enough"

Payne: What would you like to work with today?

Jane: I'm a fashion designer and I'm told by everyone that I'm very good at what I do. However, no matter how hard I try to make a big success of my work, it seems to fail. The "big break" always seems to elude me. Every time it's about to happen, it crumbles, mostly because the people I choose to do business with let me down.

Payne: Just get quiet for a moment and feel this issue in your body. Then tell me what feeling is there.

Jane: It's a simple feeling, it sounds a bit like a cliché, but the feeling is, "I'm not good enough".

Payne: Well, even clichés can be true. Does it feel true in your body?

Jane: Yes.

Payne: OK. Well, let's work with it directly and see what is revealed. Please select someone to represent yourself and also the feeling of, "I'm not good enough".

Jane takes two representatives and places them within the workshop space.

J: Jane   ING: I'm not good enough

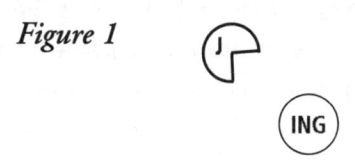

Figure 1

Payne to Jane's Representative: How are things here?

Jane's Representative: I feel uncomfortable looking at her and I have butterflies in my stomach.

Payne to "I'm not good enough": How are you here?

"I'm not good enough": I feel all sorts of things. I care about her and I don't want to let her out of my sight. I also feel ashamed, but it has nothing to do with her, it's something else.

Payne takes a representative for "shame" and places it in the constellation next to "I'm not good enough".

Payne to "I'm not good enough": How does that feel when "shame" comes in and stands next to you?

"I'm not good enough": It's very known, but I don't like it.

Payne to Jane's Representative: How is it for you when "shame" comes in?

Jane's Representative: I don't like it, I'm trembling. I feel younger, much younger, perhaps a girl, not a baby, but a girl.

Payne to Jane: Does this make any sense to you?

Jane: Yes. I know this feeling of shame.

Payne to Jane: Did anything specifically happen that made you feel ashamed when you were younger?

Jane: Well, I suppose quite a few things. Nothing comes to mind.

Payne takes a representative for "the cause" and places it in the constellation.

Payne to "The cause": How are things here?

The cause: Actually quite good. I feel a little smug. I'm a little aggressive towards her. It feels like I'm taunting her *(pointing towards "I'm not good enough")*.

Jane bursts into tears.

Payne to Jane: What is happening?

Jane: I've suddenly remembered an incident when I was about ten or eleven years old. I was pulled up in front of the class and the teacher praised me for my excellent work and said to the class that I was an example for them all to follow. I got teased terribly after that, even my best friend joined in. From then on my school work was not so good, as I didn't want to be teased like that.

Jane went on to recount how she was bullied for several days and how the friends closest to her abandoned her. In those few days, she vowed never to be in the limelight again and never to risk being humiliated in that way. Although it was a distant memory and one that did not come to mind immediately, it was clear from our work that it had left an indelible mark that had a strong influence on Jane's life and her success as a fashion designer. Her greatest fear was that after a fashion show she would read bad press reviews and would experience the humiliation all over again. The trauma entity, born out of shame, had the task of avoiding public humiliation at all costs, even though Jane herself, as the adult, wanted to take her work out to the world. Therein lays the inner conflict. Strong emotions such as shame invariably win the upper hand, and it is our task to heal that part of ourselves.

During the rest of the constellation, Jane entered into dialogue with "I'm not good enough" and "shame", re-assuring them that it won't happen again and that even if it did, they had the maturity needed to work through it.

In other work that was done with Jane, it was revealed through a Family Constellation that she had a great-grandfather who had lost a business and home. This, too, was an imprint of shame that was felt within the family system. Although it was clear that Jane's experience of being shamed at school was a large part of her fear of success, we cannot ignore the collective family imprint of shame passed down to her from her great-grandfather and his children. From observing many Family Constellations, it would seem that many of us simply re-create the experiences of our ancestors out of loyalty to them. However, it begs the question, how did Jane create the experience of other children shaming her in this way? As a dog owner, I've noticed that my animals are friendly towards confident visitors and aggressive towards those who are nervous. Perhaps Jane, unbeknownst to her, broadcast the message, "I come from a family of shame" and therefore attracted those who would respond to her subconscious message.

Chapter Four

TO WHOM DO I BELONG? – ADOPTEES

In the first book of this series, The Healing of Individuals, Families and Nations, I briefly addressed the subject of adoption. The following are some case studies based on actual clients and constellations that have taken place.

When it comes to adopted children, we must ask the question, "To whom does the child belong?" For the most part, when viewed through Family Constellation work and the revelations of the field, adopted children belong to their families of origin, their biological parents. Why is this? In essence, the child belongs to those who have given it life, irrespective of the circumstances. Another important question to ask is, "why do couples adopt?" Do they adopt for the child's reasons or their own? When couples adopt children for their own reasons, this further deepens the feeling of the adopted child that they have in some way lost their own Soul. Not only have they experienced the trauma of early childhood abandonment, but they are now expected to give something to the adoptive parents.

Charles
"I have a lot of problems with relationships"

Payne: What would you like to work with?

Charles: I am adopted and I have a lot of problems with relationships and also with my adoptive parents, particularly my mother.

Payne: Can you briefly describe the problems you are having with your adoptive parents?

Charles: Although my father is secretly supportive of my finding my biological parents, my mother is dead-set against it and will not discuss the subject.

Payne: Do your adoptive parents have other children?

Charles: No, just one other adopted child, my younger sister.

The Language of the Soul

Payne: Did they have problems conceiving a child?

Charles: Yes. My mother has a medical condition and the doctors advised her not to have any children. They tried three times and on all three occasions she had a miscarriage. It was about a year after the last miscarriage that they adopted me, and then my sister two years later.

Payne: Well, let's look at the situation more directly. Please choose representatives for each of the miscarried children, your adoptive parents, yourself and your adopted sister.

F: Father   M: Mother   AS: Adopted Sister   C: Charles
1, 2, 3: Miscarried children   PG: Paternal Grandfather
MG: Maternal Grandmother

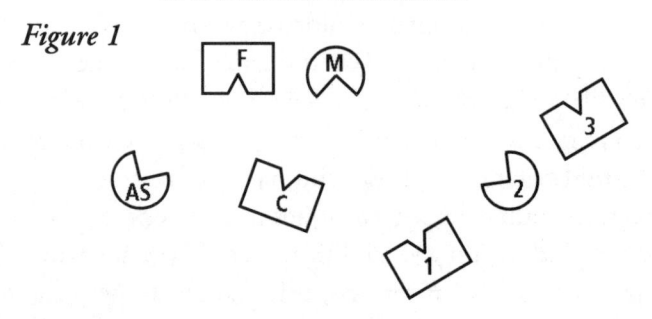

Figure 1

Payne to Adoptive Mother: How are things here?

Adoptive Mother: Heavy. I'm aware of the miscarried children but I don't want to look there.

Payne to Adoptive Father: How are things here?

Adoptive Father: I am standing next to my wife, but I also feel that I am leaning away from her slightly.

Payne to Charles's Representative: How are things here?

Charles's Representative: Unbearable. I feel the children to my right and I feel that my mother is draining energy from me. I don't want to look at her. I'm finding it quite difficult to breathe properly.

Payne to Adopted Sister: How are things here?

Adopted Sister: I really feel that I have nowhere to hide. My father looks too closely at me and I want to hold my brother's shoulder. I don't want to look at my mother, but I do feel comfortable with miscarriages here, I feel warm with them. I also feel a kind of tugging backwards from behind; it's gentle, but it's there.

Chapter Four – To Whom Do I Belong? – Adoptees

Payne moves Charles's and Adopted Sister's representatives back a little so that the miscarried children are in full view of the adoptive parents.

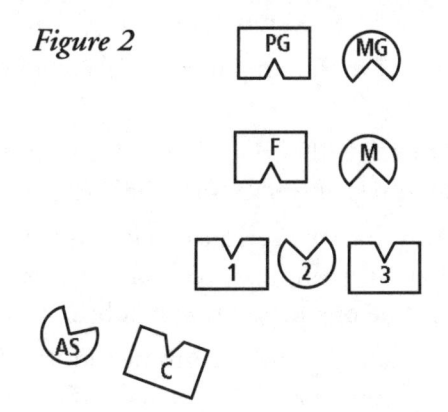

Figure 2

Payne to Adoptive Parents: How is that when you can see them more fully?

Adoptive Mother: Terrible, I want to faint.

Adoptive Father: I feel nauseous and my feeling of wanting to lean away from my wife has become stronger. I actually want to move away from her.

Payne takes a representative for Adoptive Mother's mother and Adoptive Father's father and places them behind them for support. He then moves the representatives for the miscarried children to stand directly in front of their parents.

Payne to Adoptive Parents: How is that when you see them so close to you?

The representative for the Adoptive Mother lets out a soft scream and almost falls to her knees, her mother supports her as she wails. The representative for the Adoptive Father spontaneously turns to his own father and cries on his shoulder.

Payne to Charles: Were your adoptive parents young when they got married?

Charles: *(Wiping a tear from his eye)* Yes, my father was 22 and my mother only 19. The first miscarriage took place when she was 21.

Payne: It was very difficult for them, that is clear to see. Although we have compassion for them, it was clear from the beginning of the constellation that you are a replacement for the miscarried children. That is too much of a burden for you.

Charles: Yes. I've often thought this. My mother often looks very sad, but she is always happy when she sees me.

Payne: Perhaps she is asking too much of you?

Charles: Yes, I often feel that it's my job to make her happy and to take care of her.

Payne: And your girlfriends? Do they demand the same? Or do you have the same feeling of responsibility towards them?

Charles: *(Sobs)* Always. I always seem to pick girls who have a lot of problems. My last girlfriend had alcoholic parents and she suffered from depression. The one before that had been involved in drugs.

Payne: Well, it is a pattern you are accustomed to. It seems that you learnt at a very young age that your job is to look after others and make sure that they are happy. But let us continue with the work.

Payne to Adoptive Parents: Please turn and look directly at the miscarried children once more and feel the support of your mother and father behind you.

Payne takes the first miscarried child to the mother and father.

Payne to Adoptive Parents: Please look at him and say, "It was terrible when you left, we were so much looking forward to your arrival. I now take you as our first child and give you a place in my heart".

The Adoptive Parents repeat the sentence and embrace their child.

Note: It is interesting that even though there were many women in the workshop, Charles selected male representatives for two of the miscarriages, indicating that he as an adopted boy was to take the place of one or both of the miscarried male children.

Payne takes the second miscarried child to the mother and father.

Payne to Adoptive Parents: Please look at her and say, "It was terrible when you left, we were so much looking forward to your arrival. I now take you as our second child and give you a place in my heart".

Adoptive Mother: It's more difficult for me to say this. It feels as though it is too much.

Adoptive Father: It's also more difficult for me. Like I can't go through this again.

Payne: Just feel your father and mother behind you, become more aware of their presence, and try the sentences; let's see what happens.

Chapter Four – To Whom Do I Belong? – Adoptees

Adoptive Parents to Second Child: "It was terrible when you left, we were so much looking forward to your arrival. I now take you as our second child and give you a place in my heart".

The adoptive parents embrace the second child and weep with one another. Payne now takes the third child and places him in front of his parents.

Adoptive Father: I'm angry. I can't look at him. I'm also angry with my wife and that feeling of wanting to turn away from her has come back. It feels as if this is all too much.

Adoptive Mother: I'm also angry. I want to blame my husband and I can't bear to look at this child.

Payne: Please just look at the child.

Payne allows the representatives for the parents a few moments to simply look at the third child.

Payne to Adoptive Parents: Please look at him and say, "It was terrible when you left, we were so much looking forward to your arrival. I now take you as our third child and give you a place in my heart".

Adoptive Mother: That sentence is not correct. I want to say something like, "I went insane when you left".

Payne to Adoptive Mother: Please look at your husband and say to him, "I went insane when he left".

Adoptive Mother: I went insane when he left.

Payne to Adoptive Mother: How does it feel to say that to your husband?

Adoptive Mother: It feels true and I feel softer towards him.

Payne to Adoptive Father: How does that feel when your wife says that to you?

Adoptive Father: It feels true. I'm not so angry with her any longer.

Payne: Please take the child and let him rest his head between your shoulders and make eye contact with one another.

Payne to Adoptive Parents: How does that feel now?

Adoptive Father: Much better. I feel warm towards my wife.

Adoptive Mother: It feels good to see my husband hold the child with me, it's like I'm no longer alone.

Payne: Now allow this child to stand up straight so that you can look him in the eyes and say the sentence, "It was terrible when you left, we were so much looking forward to your arrival. I now take you as our third child and give you a place in my heart".

Adoptive Parents: It was terrible when you left, we were so much looking forward to your arrival. I now take you as our third child and give you a place in my heart.

Payne: How does that feel now?

Adoptive Mother: It feels fine now. I can look at all three of them, knowing that my husband is here.

Adoptive Father: I'm sad, but OK. It feels much better.

Payne places the miscarried children in a row to the left of the parents and brings their adopted children, Charles and his sister, to stand in front of them.

Payne to Adoptive Mother: Please say to your adopted son Charles, "I am deeply sorry, I asked far too much of you. It is I who gives to you".

Payne to Charles's Representative: How does that feel?

Charles's Representative: Gosh, it's unbelievable. I feel as if a ten-ton weight has been lifted away from me. I feel good.

Payne to Adoptive Mother: How does it feel to have said that?

Adoptive Mother: There is a little guilt, but I feel much better. I'm happy for him and now I feel ready to give to him.

Payne to Adoptive Father: Please say to your adopted daughter, "I'm deeply sorry, I looked at you far too much".

Adoptive Father: I'm deeply sorry, I looked at you far too much.

Payne to Adopted Sister: How does that feel?

Adopted Sister: It's a relief.

Payne to Adoptive Father: Now say to your wife, "I'm deeply sorry, I turned away from you".

The couple spontaneously embrace as the father speaks these words. Payne then replaces Charles's representative with the client Charles.

Payne to Charles: How does it feel when you stand here now?

Charles: I feel relieved. I don't have to do anything any longer.

Payne: Please just turn towards the miscarried children and smile at them.

Charles: It feels complete when I include them in some way.

Payne: Well, in a sense, they made space for you.

Charles: Yes, I guess that's true. I've never really looked at it that way, but it feels right when you say it.

Summary

There were a couple of key elements in this constellation: firstly, the adoptive parents' inability to look at their own children; and secondly, when the adoptive mother stated that the healing sentence, "It was terrible when you left, we were so much looking forward to your arrival; I now take you as our third child and give you a place in my heart", was incorrect and that, "I went insane when you left", was a more accurate reporting of her inner feeling. What this sentence revealed was the division between the parents. Often, when a couple loses a child or children, they turn away from one another, for the grief is too much to endure.

For Charles, the *language of the Soul*, in the sentence, "I am deeply sorry, I asked far too much of you. It is I that gives to you", was pivotal in providing him with a sense of relief. Truth always provides liberation from a burden, even when that truth is at first uncomfortable to express. I have worked with many clients who have come face-to-face with their own errors in judgment, or wrongdoings, in the context of Family Constellations. However, when the language of the Soul is spoken, it is matter-of-fact, and release is experienced. The Soul does not hide behind masks; it sees everything in the light of simple truth. In essence, it sees things simply as they are. When we acknowledge feelings, events or actions from this deeper level of truth and absolute honesty and sincerity, the light of our Soul is able to penetrate through the many layers we may have built up around a given situation or story we have created. The voice is our centre of expression; therefore the *language of the Soul* connects us directly to our centre of deeper expression. When the self is expressed in this way, we notice how individuals give a sigh of relief – finally, the truth is out and acknowledged.

In Charles's case, it was clear that his parents adopted him for their reasons, and not Charles's reasons. In such cases, the adopted child no longer owns himself, or even his sense of Soul, for he has been brought into a family in order to fill a void or to replace that which has been lost. The child then feels responsible for his adoptive parents' happiness while carrying the deep wound of having been given up by his biological parents. This is indeed a heavy burden – so much so that often individuals like Charles have the feeling of having lost their Soul.

One may ask the question, "If Charles's real adoptive parents were not present in the workshop, how then does this healing work benefit him if it is only done through representatives?" Firstly, such a constellation gives Charles a clear picture of his family situation, one in which he can learn that he is not responsible for his adoptive mother's happiness. In essence, it gives him the tools and the strength to wrest himself free with respect and honour from that situation. In addition, it highlights his pattern of creating co-dependent relationships with the women he has been dating.

Secondly, as we engage in the field, we are working directly with various levels of the family unit's consciousness and awareness. I have witnessed many cases when the individuals who are *represented*, but not present, in a workshop benefit greatly from the healing process and clients report great changes on their return home. It would seem that children are much more receptive to these energetic changes. We could conclude also that, in the case of Charles, he returned to his adoptive parents feeling very different about himself and his responsibilities with that relationship. With such a big shift in self-perception, his adoptive parents could simply be responding to those changes. However, at times clients have reported back to me that their father, mother, brother, ex-husband, etc., spontaneously reported a feeling of a weight having been lifted off their shoulders on the same day my client has been present in a workshop. My advice is always to simply allow a constellation to work for you and to respect the mystery behind some of the phenomena we experience with the "field" and its greater reach.

Rowena

"I struggle with feelings about my biological mother"

Payne: What would you like to work with?

Rowena: I'm adopted and I struggle with feelings about my biological mother. I also feel guilty towards my adoptive mother for having such longings. My mother (adoptive) has been wonderful to me, very loving and kind, but I have this hole in my heart *(begins to sob)*.

Payne: How old are you, Rowena?

Rowena: 32.

Payne: Do you know anything about the circumstances behind your adoption?

Rowena: Yes, a little. All I know is that my mother was 16 years old at the

Chapter Four – To Whom Do I Belong? – Adoptees

time and she was placed in a home for unwed mothers, and it was from there that I was put up for adoption.

Payne: Do you know anything about her parents and their circumstances?

Rowena: The only thing I know is that my biological mother's father signed the adoption forms because she was under the age of 18 and therefore still a minor.

Payne: Well, we have a question then. Who gave you up for adoption? Your mother or your grandparents? It's a very valid question. Even if your mother, at the age of 16, was afraid of becoming a mother and agreed to the adoption, it is clear that the true responsibility lay with her parents. Take a moment and close your eyes. I want you to create an image in your mind of that frightened 16-year-old girl who became your mother. Do you see her?

Rowena: Yes.

Payne: How does that feel?

Rowena: I feel nothing but love for her. I have no anger in my heart, just a longing.

Payne: Good. Now place in that picture an image of your adoptive mother standing next to her and tell me how that feels.

Rowena: It feels much more relaxed than I thought.

Payne: Now say to your adoptive mother in your thoughts, "This is my mother, and I belong to her". Tell me how it feels to say that.

Rowena: It's a relief. I still feel a little guilty but much, much less than usual.

Payne instructs two women in the workshop to stand in front of Rowena where she sits and represent her biological and adoptive mothers.

Payne: Open your eyes and look at these two women. Just look.

Payne: How does it feel to look at them?

Rowena: I feel very loved by both of them.

Payne: Have you noticed how your adoptive mother smiles at your biological mother?

Rowena: Yes.

Payne: Do you know why?

Rowena: No. They don't know one another.

Payne: Ah, but they do, through you. Your mother smiles at her with gratitude for the great gift she was given. Now let us look at this deep feeling of having a hole in your heart. Look at the representative for your biological mother and say to her, "I see clearly that I was taken from you, dear Mother".

As Rowena spoke these words both Rowena and her mother's representative broke down in tears. Rowena stood up and the two women embraced, sobbing deeply. Payne takes two representatives for Rowena's biological grandparents and places them behind her mother.

Payne to Grandparents: How does this feel to be here witnessing your daughter and granddaughter embracing?

Grandmother: We've done something terrible. I have this feeling of wanting to hang my head low.

Grandfather: I don't want to look.

Payne to Rowena: Let's leave things here for now, it is enough for today. My advice is that you follow your natural impulse to find your mother.

Rowena: I started the process some time ago, but I stopped because of the guilty feelings. But this has encouraged me. I always thought that my mother had abandoned me, but it has really hit home that she was only sixteen and therefore had no choice in the matter, or even legal rights.

Payne: That's quite a big movement for you, so relish it. However, as you've seen from this work today, there will be reasons why your grandparents acted as they did.

Conclusion

When we look at Rowena's case, we must ask ourselves, Who gave up the child for adoption, her mother or her grandparents? Very often when I set up constellations to look at the case of an adopted client, there is a strong sense that the child was given up forever, with very little hope of reconciliation. This is more common, the older the birth mother was at the time of the adoption. In such cases, the adoptive parents step in to provide support. In generations gone by, much shame was attached to teenage pregnancies and pregnancies of unwed mothers. Adoptions were carried out through homes for unwed mothers and often through convents and other religious institutions. In such cases, we can also look at the birth mother as a child, for her decision-making power was removed and other adults have stepped in to make decisions for her. Very often, we see that a woman who has given up her child for adoption willingly carries within her a deep sense of wanting to die, for the burden of guilt and remorse is too heavy for her to carry. This does not necessarily mean that she is consciously suicidal, but it does mean that on one level or another she withdraws from life. When I work directly with women who have given up children for adoption, I often see that their lives have been bereft of loving, intimate relationships. Marriage often leads to divorce, or they meander from one unloving relationship to the next. This pattern would appear to stem from an internal need to punish themselves for having abandoned their child. Although this pattern can also be witnessed with women who have had abortions, it is more evident with mothers who have given up their children for adoption. A general exception seems to be when a mother gives up her child to a close family member. However, when this is done in secret and the child and others are lied to, the pattern of inner penance appears to still apply.

Belonging

Each of us, as we are born into this physical body, inherit genetic coding that has been passed down to us through countless generations of our ancestors. We are part of the collective family Soul that holds their consciousness and experiences. Brennan Healing Science has revealed that we not only have physical bodies, but also energy bodies, which in turn have concentrations of energy that form vortexes known as the chakras. These chakras not only feed the endocrine system with life force energy, but they also connect us to other people – our lovers, partners and biological family members, through what have been called relationship cords. These cords extend outwards from the chakras, linking us energetically to our parents, children and even distant ancestors. Therefore, adopted children, like all of us, feel the presence of their ancestors, whether or not they know them. There have been many stories about adopted children who have reunited with their birth parents, only to discover that they share uncanny personality traits and even the same likes and dislikes for various foods.

It has become apparent through my work with many adoptees that being adopted is indeed a heavy burden, one which seems to occupy most of their lives and becomes a life-long search for the self. When so much of ourselves is unknown, except the knowledge of not having been wanted, the burden and the wound are heavy. This does not mean to suggest that adoptees do not and cannot lead fruitful lives like anyone else, but each of my adopted clients has reported either a sense of something being missing, or a feeling of there being a hole in their heart or of having lost their Soul somewhere.

Through the many constellations I have set up for adopted individuals, the dominant theme has been to transform their relationship with their adoptive parents. As stated earlier, it is important to look at why parents adopt. Do they do so for their own reasons, or for the child's reasons? As was clear in the case of Charles, his adoptive parents were burdened by the loss of their miscarried children; thus Charles was taken as a replacement. This in itself was a heavy burden for Charles, for when we look at his adoption in the clear light of constellation work, not only was he abandoned by his birth mother, but also his adoptive parents demanded a lot from him. In this, and in many adoption cases, the adopted child is expected to give to the parents. At times, childless couples adopt children as a measure for rescuing their own marriage. I have seen many cases where the adoptive mother forms her primary emotional relationship with the adopted child as she turns away from her husband. A few years ago, I heard Bert Hellinger say that if one partner is infertile or unable to produce children and the other partner wants children, it is far better for the infertile individual to offer the other freedom through divorce. At first, I thought this was quite an extreme solution, if not a little cruel. However, in the light of some of the adopted clients I have worked with who have adoptive parents where this is the case, a divorce would seem better for everyone concerned. This is not to say that all childless couples who adopt children form unhealthy relationships with their adopted children. In order for an adopted child to have a greater sense of belonging, it behooves prospective parents to become aware of their needs, desires and motives for adoption.

Another quite controversial issue around adoption is the case of cross-racial and cross-cultural adoption. There are many poorer nations in the world that have orphanages full of unwanted children, in particular girls. In such cases, it is particularly important that the prospective adoptive parents ask themselves what they truly have to offer the child in question. In my experience, when we look at the child's needs, it is difficult to balance the two probable fates, one of being left in an orphanage in a country that has neither the resources nor the cultural imperative to care properly for the child, and the other of, the child being bereft of its original cultural identity with the exception of its physical features. In working with a number of cross-cultural adoptees, they often have a deeper sense of having lost their Souls somewhere. My advice to such parents is always to make the child's cultural heritage readily and easily available, even to actively encourage that connection. At times, adoptive parents report that their child has little or no interest in connecting with the culture of his or her origin. What should be noted here is that this very often stems from one of two motivations. There is either a loyalty to their adoptive parents which stops them, or it is owing to anger towards a culture and perhaps a country that abandoned them. In the case of cross-cultural and cross-racial adoption, we must also ask ourselves a difficult question: Is it better for the child to remain in the country or culture of their origin, despite the hardships and the difficult fate that it brings? For some, this question may seem very harsh, if not malicious; nevertheless, it is a valid question.

With all adoptions, not only cross-cultural and cross-racial adoptions, it is very important that the birth parents are honoured and deeply respected. During constellation work when I have asked adoptive parents to bow to the birth parents, and/or to their country and culture of origin, the adopted child always feels stronger with a deeper sense of self. It has always astounded me when I have heard adoptive parents say things like "Well, his mother was a drug addict", in quite a deprecating manner or "We rescued her from a life of poverty in Romania". In such cases, I remind them it was Romania (or any other country) or a drug addict that gave them such a precious gift. We must be very careful not to take a stance of superiority towards the culture or country of origin of the adoptive child. When we do so, the child is further shamed in the process. At times, I have worked with an adoptee who looks down upon his or her own culture of origin; the inner movement that I guide them through is one of honouring the origins of their life and their ancestral line. However, as previously stated, their resistance to this has often more to do with either the anger and great hurt they feel for being abandoned, or their loyalty to their adoptive parents.

The *language of the Soul* embodies an inescapable truth: "Thank you for the precious gift of this child". When we look at life's situations from the perspective of distilled truth, the *language of the Soul*, the word "but" is never expressed, for always after the "but" comes a story that lacks truth and responsibility. When we speak sentences that are divided by "but", invariably only half the sentence is really true or holds any essence of acknowledging what is; often, a sentence divided with "but" holds little or no truth at all – for example, "I love my husband, but I have little respect for him".

Whether it is an adoptive parent's attitude towards the birth parents, or a divorced person's attitude towards his or her ex-spouse, when the parent(s) are dishonoured, the child is shamed in the process.

Sam Weber

Sam Weber is one of my students who is working towards becoming a practitioner of Family Constellations. Sam is an adoptee, and here are her words:

I must have been a bitch of a baby. Not in the sense that I slept too little or cried too much, but in the sense that it took four parents to bring me into this world and then to keep me here. My mother, it would appear, was none too keen to receive my father's sperm and he, feeling an overwhelming need to deposit it, raped her. Thus was I conceived in violence.

My mother, understandably, did not welcome my conception. I was a source of pain and widespread consternation in her life. She was young, unmarried and dependent on a stepfather who was, evidently, not overly fond of her. Nevertheless, her body nurtured mine and she was delivered of me in the dead of a South African winter. Two weeks later, I was given to a new set of parents who were tasked with my general upkeep.

So it was that I grew up in a pervasive, if distant and undefined, daze of confusion as to my place of belonging in this world. Families are rather well demarcated and exclusive entities. Belonging to one generally precludes belonging to another. This simple fact caused my subconscious to balk with bewilderment. I couldn't belong to my biological family because they had ousted me. Neither could I belong to my adoptive family because I didn't share their gene pool, the very thing that defines belonging to a family. I lived my life in a subtle state of primal discomfort: if I honoured one set of parents, that honour seemed to disrespect the other.

Not that I was consciously aware of all this, growing up. I knew only that I had been adopted and that I didn't quite seem to fit in, regardless of where I was. I did not have the family nose nor did I look like Auntie Mabel or act just like Grandpa. There were no stories about my conception, my mother's pregnancy, or my birth. I had no familial medical history. I was discouraged

Chapter Four – To Whom Do I Belong? – Adoptees

from asking questions about my family of origin, maybe because my adoptive parents wanted to shield me from what they may very well have regarded as the 'awful truth' regarding my origins. Eager to fit in, I complied until after they had all died.

I eventually distanced myself sufficiently from the unhappy event of my birth and came to regard myself as never having been born at all. How I arrived here was just another part of the greater mystery of Life On Earth and something that there was no point pondering. My body, not having an origin in my mind, always seemed foreign to me. Since I had no clear sense of belonging, Earth itself was equally foreign to me. I was an alien; not from another planet, mind you, but an alien in my body, my family, and on Earth. I belonged nowhere except possibly in my own mind and in the world of spirit.

Thus bereft of roots, I dangled midair in life like an abandoned weaver bird's nest, suspended from some arbitrary twig in an unknown family tree.

Through my participation in Family Constellation work, I have come to a greater acceptance of that which is. My conception was the result of a rape. My mother gave me up for adoption. Nevertheless, as incontestable as the aforementioned are, I belong to both my father and my mother, as their child.

From my mother, my father and their ancestors, I have inherited a body, complete and whole. Both physically and emotionally, I have inherited patterns that can be regarded as good and others that can be regarded as bad. I have a genetic origin and an ancestry that stretches back through time. Regardless of the details of my conception, I am here and I am essentially a good person, no better but certainly also no worse than anybody else. I have a body and my body had a beginning as it will have an end. My conception does not define me. What defines me is what I do with the life that I received from my mother and my father. This is how it has always been between parent and child and now I know that it is true for me, too. My honour for my biological parents is not dependent on the circumstances of my life.

From my adoptive parents I received love, nurturing and care. They clothed me, housed me, fed me, protected me and educated me. They gave me every opportunity in life that I could possibly have wished for. They were always there for me, even during the times that I perplexed them as much as I sometimes did myself. They always did their very best for me. This is how it has always been between parent and child and now I know that it is true for me, too. My honour for my adoptive parents is not dependent on belonging to their gene pool.

My involvement with Family Constellation work has also affected my romantic relationships. It used to be difficult for me to accept love. It used to be that I always pushed, always tested to see how long it would last. However much love was given to me, it was never quite enough to be convincing. It was never as intimate as I wanted it to be and I always ended up withdrawing into myself in a misguided attempt at lonely self-sufficiency. That special bond that I was looking for, the one that I should have had with my mother, was nowhere to be found. No one could love me the way I so desperately wanted to be loved, the way my mother should have loved me.

As I have gained a stronger sense of self through family constellation work, I no longer look to my partner to fulfill my expectations of my mother. I am learning to be in the relationship as an equal, to receive love without incessant questioning and to trust that it will last for as long as it should. I am more present in all my relationships, less entangled in past predicaments and future fears. Ironically, I have now found the sense of self-sufficiency that eluded me so painfully for so many years.

My journey through family constellation work has been one of deep healing, not only through work done in my own constellations but also through representing for others. As a society, our stories do not really differ that much. We all suffer loss and experience love. We all lose our way from time to time. Through participating in Family Constellations we get the unique opportunity to stand in each other's shoes, however briefly, and to see a reflection of ourselves in the eyes of others. Slowly the beautiful realisation dawns that ultimately we are all part of the greater family of humanity; ultimately we all, without exception or exclusion, belong to one another.

I am no longer an alien. I am Sam Weber, originally Susan Putter. I belong.

A final word on adoption

As discussed in my first book on Family Constellation work, *The Healing of Individuals, Families and Nations,* the effects of adoption can be far-reaching and trans-generational in nature. Family Constellation work has revealed what have been termed the "Orders of Love". The Orders of Love describe a natural hierarchy, a distinct order that states who belongs and who doesn't belong. In observing work with clients during the process of Family Constellations, we see an undeniable and almost measurable effect when the Orders of Love have been disrupted in some families. The Orders of Love prescribe who comes first, who belongs after that, and describe a natural flow of love from grandparents to parents and to children. These orders span countless generations but tend to be experienced as having the greatest influence within three to seven generations.

Within the Orders of Love, the parents give, and children take. However, disruptions to these Orders can take place when there has been an early death of a parent, grandparent, child or infant – caused by wars and other tragedies, family secrets and many other events where individuals are either missing or excluded. Many of the feelings associated with being adopted (for example: deep sadness, depression, a sense of something being missing, or a sense of having lost one's Soul) can be passed down from generation to generation. On a few occasions, I have worked with clients who have reported a deep sense of not belonging to their families and have often wondered if they had been adopted, despite the fact that they share many physical characteristics with their family. On investigation, we have learnt that a grandparent or great-grandparent was either given up for adoption or spent most of their childhood in an orphanage, having no sense of where and to whom they belonged. When we look back just two or three generations, we find that many of us have grandparents or great-grandparents who were either adopted or spent their childhoods in orphanages. This was largely owing to poverty, or in the case when a mother died, society frowned upon or did not allow a man to care for his children and it was thought better for the children to be sent to an orphanage. Widows, too, were often forced to give up their children for adoption or place them in orphanages as they invariably did not have careers or an income that could support them. More often than not, the only way they could keep their children was to marry quickly after the death of their husband; however, there was no guarantee that their new husband wanted to have another man's child in his household.

It is important to remember that we do not live in the isolation that the boundary of our physical body may have us believe. On a subconscious and energetic level, we belong to family groups, and whatever our ancestors experienced is transferred to us through the collective family Soul to which we belong. Family Constellation work has revealed countless times that most of the emotions and disruptive life patterns we are dealing with originate

The Language of the Soul

from our family system rather than from direct personal experience. Science, in a relatively new field of genetics called epigenetics, is beginning to uncover evidence that suggests that what our grandparents experienced is passed down to us biologically. Epigenetics is defined as the transmission of non-DNA sequence information.

Family Constellation work is a blend of psychotherapeutic process, energy and Soul work that resonates with echoes of shamanism and has been proven to alleviate many difficulties and challenges that are trans-generational in nature.

Chapter Five

ADDICTIONS AND SUBSTANCE ABUSE: RELIEVING A HOLE IN THE SOUL

Over the past few years, I have worked with a number of individuals who have struggled with one form or another of substance abuse. At times, it is not the addicted individual who attends a workshop, but a sibling, spouse or parents of such individuals.

What I have observed is that the individual who is addicted to drugs appears to be the member of the family that embodies and "acts out" the family's unexpressed pain and grief. In principle, their feelings in the affairs of another family member are no different to feelings any one of us could have inherited from parents, grandparents and the like; however, it would appear that the events and feelings they are entangled in tend to be of a weightier nature. Quite often with drug addiction, we do see that one or more members of the extended family are suicidal, either consciously or on a deeper level. "Not being alive" and being actively suicidal are two sides of the same coin; a yearning to be with the dead can be expressed in many different ways.

Francesca
"My brother is addicted to heroine"

Payne to Francesca: What would you like to work with?

Francesca: My brother has asked me to set up a proxy constellation for him as he is unable to attend this workshop. I believe he called you during the week giving his permission for me to do this work on his behalf.

Payne: Yes, he did, and we had a brief chat. He is addicted to heroine, is that correct?

Francesca: Yes, he has been a drug addict since he was in his late teens and has been on various drugs, from marijuana to cocaine and heroine. It is really beginning to take its toll on his body and I'm very concerned for him.

Payne: How many children are there in your family and where does Michael fall in the order?

Francesca: Michael is the eldest, and then it is me, then my younger sister. There are three of us in total, and no miscarriages or abortions, as far as I know.

Payne: Are your parents still married?

Francesca: Yes.

Payne: Any incidents of note in the family?

Francesca: No, nothing out of the ordinary, no tragedies.

Payne: Please tell me a little about both your mother's and your father's families of origin.

Francesca: My father is one of three boys, nothing extraordinary there. I checked with him and asked him all the relevant questions before I came here today. However, my mother's mother died when my mum was six years old. I also checked further back in her family history, but she did not know of anything else significant apart from my grandmother's death.

Payne: So, apart from your grandmother dying early, there are no other early deaths in your family?

Francesca: None.

Payne: How did your grandmother die, do you know that?

Francesca: My mother told me that she is not certain, but she believed it was pneumonia.

Payne: Well, let us set up a constellation. Please select representatives for your mother, your father, yourself, your grandmother, your grandfather, and your brother, Michael. I've included you in this constellation, as you are the one present in the workshop, although the constellation is for Michael. It is important that we look at anything that you may be carrying for Michael.

Francesca: Thank you. I appreciate that, and I think it is quite important, too.

Francesca looks around the room and selects representatives according to her impulse and places them on the workshop floor as she follows her inner feeling.

Chapter Five – Addictions and Substance Abuse

GF: Grandfather   GM: Grandmother   M: Mother   F: Father
Fr: Francesca   Mi: Michael

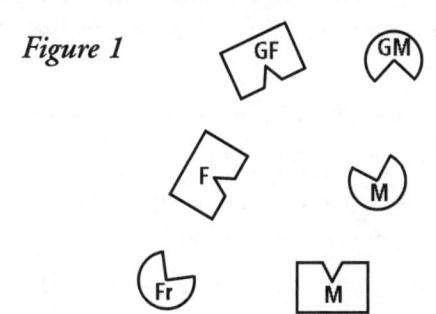

Figure 1

Immediately as the constellation is set up, Payne notices that Michael's representative is shaking visibly.

Payne to Michael's Representative: What is happening here?

Michael's Representative: I'm shaking. I have the feeling that I want to fall to my knees and I can't keep my eyes off my grandmother. I feel a deep pain.

Payne to Mother: How are things with you?

Mother: I feel totally numb. I can see my own mother through the corner of my eye, but I can't look at her.

Payne to Grandfather: How are things here?

Grandfather: I feel dead. This is too much to bear.

Payne to Father: How are things with you?

Father: I am deeply concerned for my son, but otherwise, I'm not involved in this story. I do feel estranged from my wife; she doesn't seem to be with me at all.

Payne to Francesca's Representative: How are things here with you?

Francesca's Representative: Not good. I feel torn between standing next to my father, where it would seem to be safer, and helping my brother. I don't want to look at my mother or my grandmother. It's too much for me.

Payne to Mother: Please turn and look at your mother and tell me what happens.

Mother: I am very sad, more than sad, distraught. I want to go to her. I really want to go to her.

Michael's Representative: I want to go with her.

The Language of the Soul

Payne instructs both representatives to follow their impulse. Grandmother's representative spontaneously lies on the floor and both Michael's representative and his mother kneel beside her. Mother sobs loudly and Michael places his arms around her to comfort her.

Payne to Francesca the Client: What else happened? What was your mother's fate after her mother died?

Francesca: She was taken away to live with an aunt, both her and her sister. Her brother stayed with her father.

Payne: Did your mother go to her mother's funeral?

Francesca: No. My mother told me that she remembers the doctor coming to the house to visit her very sick mother and on that very same day she was sent to her aunt's house. She never saw her mother again.

Payne to Michael's Representative: Please say to you mother, "I will go, so that you can stay with the other children".

Michael's Representative: *(Confidently)* I will go so that you can stay with the other children.

Payne to Francesca: He is doing it for your mother. She wishes to leave so that she can be with her mother, but she can't, so Michael is volunteering to go in her place. That is a great act of love on his part, a misguided one, but a great act of love, nonetheless.

Payne asks the representative for Michael and Francesca's grandmother to stand up so that the two women can face one another. The women weep together.

Payne to Mother: Say to your mother, "Beloved Mother, it was so difficult when you left and all I wanted was to be with you".

Mother: Yes, that's true, that's all I've ever wanted.

Payne to Mother: Please try and say the words, look in her eyes when you say it.

Mother: Beloved Mother, it was so difficult when you left and all I wanted was to be with you.

Payne to Mother: How does that feel?

Mother: It's wonderful; I just want to be with her.

Payne to Grandmother: Please say to your daughter, "Beloved daughter, one day we shall be together, when it is your proper time. Meanwhile, go to your husband and children; that is where you belong".

Chapter Five – Addictions and Substance Abuse

Grandmother: Beloved daughter, one day we shall be together, when it is your proper time. Meanwhile, go to your husband and children; that is where you belong.

Payne to Grandmother: How was it to say that?

Grandmother: Easy.

Payne to Mother: And for you?

Mother: It was very strange when she talked about my husband and children; it is like it is new information for me.

Payne to Mother: Please turn and look at your son, your daughter and your husband and tell me how that feels.

Mother: Really strange. They are almost like strangers to me, but not, at the same time.

Payne to Mother: Please look directly at Michael and say to him whilst pointing towards your mother, "This is my mother, she left us early and I have missed her very much. Leave the grief with me; I will take care of it".

Mother: This is my mother, she left us early and I have missed her very much. Leave the grief with me; I will take care of it.

Payne to Michael's Representative: How does that feel?

Michael's Representative: I don't believe her.

Mother: He's right; I don't quite believe myself either when I say those words.

Payne takes Michael's and Francesca's representatives and stands them next to their father.

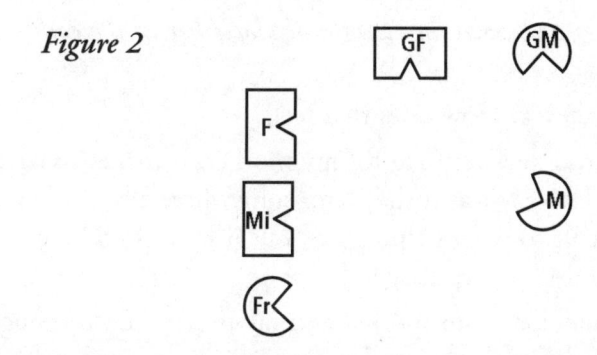

Figure 2

Payne to Father: Please look at your son and say to him, "It is safer next to me".

Father: It is safer next to me.

Payne to Father: How did that feel?

Father: Good, but I feel frustrated. It's like I've been powerless all this time to do anything.

Payne to Michael's Representative: How did it feel to hear that? And how does it feel to stand next to your father in this way?

Michael's Representative: I believed him, and it feels good to stand next to him. It's very new, but I'm still looking at my mother and I still have this pull to help her.

Payne to both Father and Francesca's Representative: Say to your son and brother, "Please stay, and leave mother's business with her".

Michael's representative flings his arms around his father and sister and sobs.

Payne to Michael's Representative: What happened here?

Michael's Representative: When they said, "Please stay", I felt a wave of emotion come over me. It's like I don't have to do it all alone anymore.

Payne to Michael's Representative: Please look over to your mother and say to her, "Dear Mother, the best place for me is next to Father".

Michael's Representative: Dear Mother, the best place for me is next to Father.

Payne: How does that feel?

Michael's Representative: I still feel sad that she is there all alone, but it feels very good to be next to my father and I love my sister a lot.

Payne: Yes, your sister loves you a lot, too.

Payne takes Francesca the client and places her in the constellation in place of her representative.

Payne to Francesca: How does that feel?

Francesca: I, too, feel very sad for my mother. It makes so much sense to me; I've always felt as if she were "somewhere else". It's very sad. It's very difficult to resist helping her, but it feels good here with my brother and father, really good.

Payne: Please look at your mother and say to her, "Even though I stand with Father, I remain your daughter".

Francesca: Even though I stand with Father, I remain your daughter.

Payne: How does that feel now?

Francesca: Better, much better. I love my mother but I know that there is nothing I can do.

Payne: The first time you worked with a constellation, we worked on the matter of your divorce; perhaps you would like to work further on this topic at some later stage.

Francesca: Yes, I think it is important. I hope this helps my brother, but I sense it is not entirely complete.

Payne: No, it isn't. We can do more, but not today. We have done enough for now.

The constellation ends.

Conclusion

With this and other constellations on the subject of heroine addiction, we invariably see that one or more members of a family system are suicidal. In Michael's case, his mother had a deep feeling of wanting to follow her own mother into the world of the dead and so Michael, through his heroine addiction, was saying, "Mother, I will go in your place". In every case of heroine addiction I have worked with, the heroine addict is either suicidal, representing the suicidal feelings of another in the family, offering to die on behalf of someone else, or following another directly into death. Although such dynamics can show up in almost any family system, with or without drug addiction present, heroine addiction, in my experience, is specifically related to an inclination to die.

If you know someone who is addicted to heroine, it may not be immediately obvious where this inclination to die may stem from. The dynamic and the events that are the origin of this impulse to follow the dead may have occurred two, three, or more generations earlier.

Whilst many drug rehabilitation and 12-step programs are successful in assisting some heroine addicts to come off this destructive drug, what is very important is that the entire family system is investigated and preferably worked with directly. Often parents are left clueless and feeling helpless when their child has such an addiction, for they themselves are unaware of their, or their parents', childhood experiences. The feelings entangled within them can be passed down to the very children they have difficulty in understanding. I've heard many a parent explain through exasperation what a perfect childhood their son and daughter had – a stable home, good schooling, loving parents, sufficient income – and they simply do not understand how or why this has happened to their child. Often they are racked with guilt trying to figure what they did wrong. Not until the revelation within the "field" and the *language of the Soul* tells the real tale behind their child's plight can they begin the healing process, which will involve both the parents and the child. However, sadly, for some, it is easier, even after being exposed to family constellation work, to simply allow their child to carry the burden alone than to face their own demons. I doubt very much if this happens out of callousness, but when faced with the task of dealing with a much bigger picture than they thought, it is often times more reassuring to follow the guidelines of traditional therapies than to branch out in the unknown.

Several weeks after Michael's constellation took place, Francesca called me to say that although her brother was still using marijuana, he had come off heroine of his own accord without the assistance of a rehabilitation program and he reported feeling much lighter.

Sarah
"Smoking marijuana"

Payne: What would you like to work with?

Sarah: I have quite a severe addiction to marijuana. It took quite a lot for me not to have a joint this morning before coming.

Payne: How long have you had this problem?

Sarah: I'm now 28 and I've been smoking marijuana since I was about 16. At first it was about once a week, then it became more frequent, and by the time I was 19 it was every day, and nowadays it is two to three times a day. Most people don't notice it, except when it interferes with my sleep patterns. At times I stay up all night and then can't get out of bed in the morning, or I sleep for eleven or twelve hours on the trot.

Payne: Have there been periods in your life when you have been sober?

Sarah: Yes, once, I met a very nice man and I gave up whilst we were dating as I knew he wasn't into dope at all and I liked him. But when tensions began to rise in the relationship owing to other issues, I began smoking again. Occasionally I do go one or two days without it, but not often.

Chapter Five – Addictions and Substance Abuse

Payne: What happens when you are sober?

Sarah: I feel stressed out, sometimes aggressive. It's like the world and my feelings become overwhelming for me. I have a feeling of not belonging, which is a feeling I also have when I'm smoking.

Payne: Please tell me about your family of origin, your parents and siblings, etc.

Sarah: I have two sisters and a brother. I'm the second eldest, my brother is the youngest, he's only 17.

Payne: Do any of your siblings have any detectable problems as far as you know?

Sarah: My eldest sister has also had some drug-related problems, but we don't communicate that much. My younger siblings all seem fine to me. My brother is a bit of a loner, he doesn't seem to have any friends.

Payne: Are your parents still married?

Sarah: Yes.

Payne: Any miscarriages that you know of?

Sarah: I think my mother had one just before my youngest brother came.

Payne: Please tell me about both of your parents' families of origin in terms of who is in them, significant events, early deaths, tragedies, etc.

Sarah: My father was one of three children; he has a brother and a sister. His parents lived into their late eighties. My mother's family is a little different. My mum is one of five children. She's the youngest, and she had a twin sister who died of an illness just a month or two after birth.

Payne: So in fact there were six children?

Sarah: Well, from what I know, there was also another child who died, a boy, I think.

Payne: What do you know about him?

Sarah: I think he came even after my mother. He was premature and my mother came from a poor family and they didn't have proper medical care in those days.

Payne: Where is your mother's family from?

Sarah: Originally from Portugal. My parents got married at an early age in Portugal and then emigrated to South Africa in their early twenties.

The Language of the Soul

Payne: Well, let's set up a constellation to look at your family. Please choose representatives for yourself, your mother, her twin sister, and her baby brother who was born prematurely.

Sarah looks around the room and selects representatives according to her impulse and places them on the workshop floor in a pattern that has meaning to her. Payne notices that tears begin to roll down her face before she is complete.

Payne to Sarah: What is happening?

Sarah: As I began to place my mother's twin sister, I felt overwhelmed with grief. It feels as if I miss her.

Payne: Continue to set up the constellation as best you can and I'll work with your representative.

M: Mother   T: Twin Sister/Aunt   S: Sarah
GG: Great Grandmother   GF: Grandfather   GM: Grandmother   B: Brother

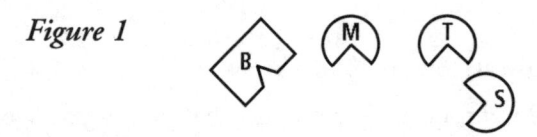

Figure 1

Payne: The first thing I notice is that your representative is standing very close to your mother's twin sister. But let me investigate.

Payne to Sarah's Representative: How are things here?

Sarah's Representative: I feel almost hypnotized. I'm transfixed by my mother's twin sister, it's like I want to be her, or be a part of her, it's strange... actually, I feel kind of stoned.

Payne to Mother: How are things with you?

Mother: I feel very weak, almost like a fainting feeling. I'm afraid that if I look at my twin I may come apart at the seams.

Payne to Twin Sister: How are things with you?

Twin Sister: I'm very happy to be standing next to my sister. I'm a little sad, but otherwise OK.

Payne to Brother: How are things for you?

Brother: Actually, I'm not here. I feel good, but I'm really not here.

Payne: Let's bring in the parents.

Chapter Five – Addictions and Substance Abuse

Payne takes two representatives for Sarah's Portuguese grandparents and places them in the constellation behind the twins. As Sarah's grandmother enters the constellation, she covers her face and between her sobs she cries, "It's too much, it's too much". Payne then places a representative for her mother (Sarah's great-grandmother) behind her and she calms down.

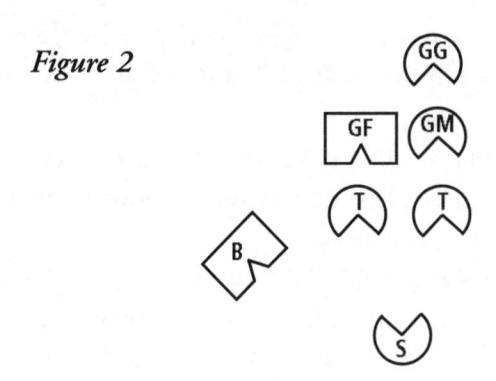

Figure 2

Payne asks the twin sisters to turn and face their parents.

Payne to Mother: How is it to stand looking at your parents?

Mother: Difficult. There is a lot of sadness and I still can't dare to look at my twin sister.

Payne: Please turn slightly and try to look at her.

As the representative for Sarah's mother turns to look at her twin sister, she wails with grief and throws her arms around her sister. Her twin supports her as her heavy tears bring her to the verge of collapsing. Her twin cries along with her and then their mother, followed shortly by the father, spontaneously move forward to hold both girls. Sarah's great-grandmother also moves in closer to support the huddled group.

Payne to Sarah the client: How are you doing?

Sarah: It's terrible to see my mother in so much pain, but she lost her twin. So many things make sense to me now, her sadness. I always thought she was homesick for Portugal.

Payne: She is homesick for Portugal, but really for who was lost there, her twin sister.

Payne to Mother: Now that you are more settled, please look directly into your sister's eyes and say to her, "It's a great pity that you couldn't stay, I've longed for you".

Mother: It's a great pity that you couldn't stay *(loud sobbing commences again)*... I've longed for you.

Payne to Mother: Please just breathe deeply and feel your sister, allow yourself to feel very present with her.

Payne to Sarah's Representative: How are things with you now?

Sarah's Representative: I no longer feel hypnotized, I'm very sad, but I feel much more present. It really touches me to see my mother with her sister.

The representative for Sarah's grandfather spontaneously reaches out for his son (Sarah's mother's brother who was born prematurely and died) and brings him into the group hug.

Sarah's Representative: Oh, that feels much better. I feel even more present, still sad, but it is like I suddenly woke up even more from a deep sleep. Each movement is making a difference.

Once the family group is calm, the tears are gone and they are smiling at one another, Payne turns the representative for Sarah's mother to face Sarah's representative directly.

Payne to Sarah's Representative: Please say to your mother, "I did it out of love for you, dear Mother".

Sarah's Representative: *(Wiping a tear from her eye)* I did it out of love for you, dear Mother.

Payne: How does it feel when you say that?

Sarah's Representative: True. It was almost as if my aunt was my own twin sister and I was searching for her. It was a very strange feeling, here yet not here, in a dream world and my aunt was the only thing I could see.

Payne: Thank you, you can take your seat now, I will work with Sarah directly.

Payne to Sarah: How do you feel?

Sarah: If you had told me that my marijuana smoking was to do with my mother's twin I would have thought you were crazy, but this is so real to me, all the feelings, the grief. I've always sensed my mother's sadness, it has always been there.

Payne: Now say to your mother, "Dear Mother, every puff of marijuana was for you, and I did it with love".

Chapter Five – Addictions and Substance Abuse

Sarah: *(Sarah tries to compose herself)* Sure, this is difficult. It feels that if I say those words, I will cry for a thousand years. There's a huge tidal wave of emotion inside of me.

Payne gently places his hand in the small of Sarah's back to offer his support.

Payne: Just try to say the words and allow whatever feelings want to come to be present.

Sarah: Dear Mother………….. every puff of marijuana………. was for you………… and I did it with love.

Sarah rushes to her mother and flings her arms around her. Her mother gently runs her fingers through her hair as Sarah cries into her bosom.

Payne: Please look at your mother and say to her, "I leave my aunt, your sister, with you".

Sarah: I leave my aunt, your sister, with you.

Payne: Now turn to your aunt and say to her, "Beloved Aunt, it's a pity that you couldn't stay. Please wait for me patiently and I will come when it is my proper time, and not one moment before".

Sarah: Beloved Aunt, it's a pity that you couldn't stay. Please wait for me patiently and I will come when it is my proper time, and not one moment before.

Payne: How does that feel now?

Sarah: It's very good to see my aunt and I can leave her where she is.

Payne: Good. Our work is done for today.

They return to their chairs.

Payne to Sarah: Now that we've uncovered the underlying dynamic that is the cause of your marijuana addiction, you'll have to choose a time when you want to tackle the physical problem. Your body has become accustomed to the drug and it may take a while for you to kick the habit; however, it may not.

Sarah: Well, now I know where it comes from, sadness. I have more to work with. I feel so much clearer than ever before, which is quite something for a pothead! *(Everyone in the workshop laughs along with Sarah)*

Payne: Thank you for your courage. Our work is done.

Summary

Sarah quite rightly said, "If you had told me that my marijuana smoking was to do with my mother's twin, I would have thought you were crazy". Who would have thought it? When tragedies occur within families, deep emotions become enmeshed in the family Soul and all other members feel them, even a generation or more later, depending very much on the scale of the trauma. Sarah did reveal that in some earlier therapy she had done, she had uncovered a feeling of being abandoned by her mother, which in a sense is true, as her mother was searching for her twin sister. However, when we approach subjects with Family Constellation work, a much bigger and more accurate picture is revealed that is based on *events* and not on feelings. Feelings lend themselves to interpretation and when we carry feelings that make no sense to us, we then search for the meaning and origin of those feelings – hence, stories like "my mother has abandoned me" come to life. We can spend many years trying to resolve a feeling that is based on a story that is either totally untrue, in part true, or not the complete picture.

Many of the marijuana addicts and regular users I have worked with have an "other worldly" feel to them. Many of them are also involved in alternative lifestyles, metaphysics and alternative spirituality. When not in balance with day-to-day life, alternative spirituality and metaphysics can also be a sign of searching for that which is in the other world, the world of the dead. However, the "that" is always a "who". Mind-altering substances take us away from this world to the boundaries of another world, the world of the dead. When it comes to drug addiction of any sort, we must always ask ourselves, "Who is missing?" The answers are always there, and as we begin to heal the hole in the family Soul, the hole in our own Soul will begin to heal.

At times, regular users of marijuana who are also involved in alternative spirituality have argued that shamans and medicine men use such substances as part of spiritual rituals. However, it is important to note that such shamanic practices take years of apprenticeship under rigorous supervision and are by no means a casual affair.

Chapter Five – Addictions and Substance Abuse

Tim

"My drinking has become a problem"

Payne: What would you like to work with?

Tim: I'm 38 years old and I've been quite a heavy drinker since I was about 16. It has caused problems in my life over the years with drunk-driving offences, relationships ending because of it, and now it has taken more control of my life. I basically spend from Friday to Sunday totally drunk and now during the week it is beginning to take more hold.

Payne: Would you consider yourself an alcoholic?

Tim: I don't like to admit it, but I'm forced to, the evidence is there.

Payne: Are you sober now?

Tim: Yes, I tried to drink as little as possible yesterday because I knew I had to be sober for this event.

Payne: Thank you, I appreciate that. Please tell me a little about your life, the significant events. For example, has anyone close to you died? Anyone in the family?

Tim: No, only my grandmother, and that was when I was 22.

Payne: Please tell me about your family of origin in terms of who is in it, and miscarriages, your mother's family and your father's family.

Tim: I have one brother and a sister, I am the eldest child. As far as I know, my mother did not have any miscarriages. My parents are still married.

Payne: Did either of them have any other marriages or significant relationships prior to their marriage?

Tim: No, they were 23 or 24 when they married. No doubt they had boyfriends or girlfriends before, but nothing significant that I know of.

Payne: Please tell me about your parents' families.

Tim: My father's father, my grandfather, was killed in an accident when my father was only 16 years old. He was also the eldest child and he had to go out to work in order to support the family. He had two sisters and a baby brother.

Payne: That's quite a tragedy in the family.

Tim: My father rarely speaks of it; my mother has told me most of the story.

Payne: And your mother's family?

Tim: Nothing out of the ordinary that I know of. I do know that her great-grandmother died quite young and that her great-grandfather re-married, but other than that, no one else died, apart from in old age.

Payne: OK, let's take a moment. Please just close your eyes and I want you to imagine that your father's father, your grandfather, is standing in front of you. It doesn't matter whether you know what he looks like or not, just imagine him there, or simply have a thought of him if you are not particularly visual, and tell me what happens.

Tim: I can see him clearly. I remember a photo of him coming back from a hunting trip; he had a rabbit in his hand.

Payne: OK, just sit in silence with this image and let us see what happens.

Tim: I feel sad; it's more of a longing.

Payne: Where do you feel him in your body?

Tim: My lungs.

Payne: And what feeling is in your lungs if you put all of your focus there?

Tim: A deeper sadness, also an emptiness, it's quite palpable.

Payne: OK, let's work more directly with this. Please choose a representative for yourself, your father and your grandfather.

Tim chooses three representatives from the workshop attendees and places them according to his feeling.

Payne: The first thing I notice is that your father's back is to you and that your representative is looking directly at your grandfather

Tim: I simply placed them according to my feeling; I don't really know what it means. But I do feel that my father's back is towards me. I think he is disappointed in me because my career has never really taken off. I don't think he knows about the drinking.

Payne: It is better that we don't get into the story, but we simply look at the underlying truths of this relationship.

Payne steps into the "field" in order to investigate.

Payne to Father: How are things here?"

Father: I feel quite small, and very fidgety. I don't want to look at my

Chapter Five – Addictions and Substance Abuse

father directly and I feel very heavy. I have the feeling that I want to close my eyes and curl up and go to sleep. It's a bit much for me here.

Payne to Grandfather: How do you feel?

Grandfather: I feel sad, very sad. I'm trying to look at my son, but he won't look at me. I notice my grandson and it is good to see him.

Payne to Tim's Representative: How are things here with you?

Tim's Representative: I have a strange magnetic pull towards my grandfather but I'm more concerned that my father's back is towards me. I want to be able to see him.

Payne walks to Father and turns him around so that he can see his son.

GF: Grandfather   F: Father   T: Tim   GM: Grandmother/mother

Figure 1

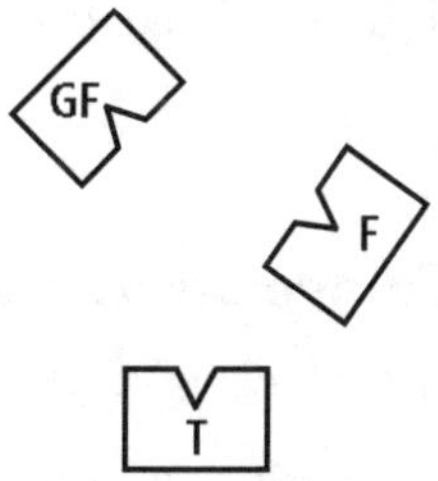

Payne to Father: How is that now?

Father: There is heat behind me and I feel pulled to turn back the way that I was.

Payne to Father: And when you look at your son?

Father: I can't look at him, something about his eyes.

Payne to Father: OK, turn back around.

Payne to Tim the Client: Do you look like your grandfather?

Tim: Yes, somewhat.

Payne: Ah, we see this often. Your father cannot look at you as you remind him of the pain of losing his father at a time when a boy most needs his father. He was 16, therefore on the bridge between boyhood and manhood. Does that make sense to you?

Tim: *(Wiping a tear from his eye)* Yes, well, not logically, but I remember so many times when I caught my father looking at me strangely, then he would become very aloof.

Payne: Well, let me continue. We'll see if we can find some resolution here.

Payne to Father: Please look directly at you father and tell me what happens.

Father: It's very difficult.

Payne takes a representative for his mother and places her next to him as support.

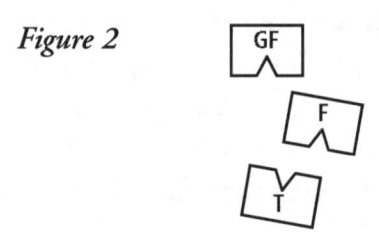

Figure 2

Payne to Father: How does that feel now with your mother standing beside you?

Father: Much better.

Payne to Mother/Grandmother: And how are you?

Mother/Grandmother: Very sad, but I'm here for my son.

Payne to Father: Please look at your father again.

The representative for Tim's father lifts his head and looks directly at his father. His chest heaves and he releases a lot of grief. His mother gently walks him over to his father and his father embraces him. Meanwhile, Tim's representative releases the same kind of grief with a heaving chest.

Payne to Tim's Representative: How are things with you?

Tim's Representative: I feel so much grief. It's almost as if it was my own father who had died. I'm happy to see him there with his father, but I can't reach him.

Payne to Tim's Representative: We'll get there, step by step.

Payne to Tim the Client: How is it for you to be watching this?

Tim: A lot of sadness. It feels exactly as my representative said, like I lost my own father.

Payne to Grandfather: Please look your son in the eyes and say, "Beloved Son, I'm sorry that I had to leave; it was my fate, but I remain you father".

Grandfather: My dear, dear boy, I'm still your father.

Chapter Five – Addictions and Substance Abuse

Payne to Grandfather: I noticed you changed the healing sentence.

Grandfather: Ever since I looked at him, the words, "My dear, dear boy" were in my head.

Payne to Father: How was that to hear your father speak to you?

Father: Wonderful. Those words, "dear, dear boy" meant a lot to me.

Payne to Father: Please look at your father and say to him, "Beloved Father, it's a pity you left so early, please wait for me patiently, there is still much work for me here".

Father: Dad, please wait for me patiently, I still have a lot of work here to do.

Payne to Workshop: This is the power of the "field". Even though as a facilitator I listen for the healing sentence, the representatives know better. There was a much deeper connection with this spontaneous change in the wording.

Payne to Grandfather: *(Laughing)* Er…do you know what to say next? Or should I suggest the sentence? *(Both men laugh)* OK, please say to your son whilst you point at your grandson, "Look, you have a son, and he needs you in the same way you needed me".

Grandfather to Father: Look, you have a son, and he needs you in the same way you needed me.

Father lifts his head off his father's shoulder and looks at his son across the room. He has a look of surprise in his eyes.

Payne to Father: What happens when you look at your son?

Father: Those words, "your son", were like new information to me. I feel almost surprised that I have a son.

Payne asks Tim's representative to sit down and he brings Tim the client into the constellation and walks him across to his father. The three men embrace. Payne instructs Tim to lay his head sideways on his father's chest with his mouth wide open towards his father's heart.

Payne to Tim: Keep your mouth open and breathe in your father's heart. Take nice deep breaths and continue until you feel "full" of your father.

This process took about three minutes or so and the two men continued to deepen their embrace.

Tim: I don't want to let go of him. I've longed for this my whole life.

The Language of the Soul

Payne: Just enjoy it and continue to breathe him in. Breathe him in until you feel him right down to your feet and in every part of your body.

Payne to Tim: Now say to your father, "Every drink was for you and Grandfather".

Tim: Whoa… *(Tim breaks down and sobs deeply again.)*

Payne: Just try to say the words.

Tim: Every drink was for you and Grandfather.

Payne: How does that feel now?

Tim: It's a relief to have finally said it.

Payne: OK, we're not quite finished here.

Payne places Tim with his back to his father, leaning gently against him, and places Grandfather behind Father so that the three generations of men stand in a row.

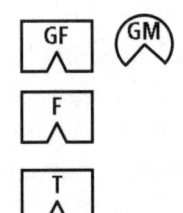

Figure 3

```
GF    GM
 F
 T
```

Payne to Tim: Just lean a little against your father and feel the support. How does it feel?

Tim: It feels great. New, very new, but very good.

Payne: Enjoy that for a moment and then let's return to the chair.

Payne to Tim: How does it feel now it's over?

Tim: I feel a little shaky, but I feel good.

Payne: You are bound to feel a little shaky, that was a lot of emotion you released back there.

Tim: Yes. I was quite surprised at how deep the feelings were.

Payne: With regards to your drinking, you may still need some assistance to kick that habit; after all, your body has a physical addiction, too, now. But let's not make any predictions. I would like to suggest that you follow a twelve-step program, or find yourself a professional mentor who will help you release the need for alcohol.

Chapter Five – Addictions and Substance Abuse

Tim: Should I stop drinking immediately?

Payne: That's up to you, but realize that your physical body may have different ideas for a little while. I would like to suggest that when you do drink, raise your glass and say "To Father and Grandfather". In that way, you will bring more into consciousness the work we have done today. Please keep in touch and let me know your progress.

Tim: Oh, I'll do more than that. I have other issues I want to work with so I'll be back.

Payne: Well, Rome was not built in a day, so let's talk further about the next steps for you.

Conclusion

What Family Constellation work has often revealed to us is that alcoholism is frequently an expression of "searching for the missing father". The dynamic is very often trans-generational in nature. As in Tim's case, it was not his own father who was missing, but his grandfather. However, on a deeper level, Tim's own father was also "missing" in a way, as he was pre-occupied with his own missing father. With this work, general patterns have been observed and as human relationships and family systems can be very complex, I feel that it would be unwise to make it a firm rule that alcohol abuse is always about the search for the father, or that there is a missing father somewhere in the extended family system. To date, though, constellation work has shown me this pattern repeatedly. Having said that, each case and each client must be approached as an individual, with no pre-conceived ideas of what is. Because Family Constellations engage in *the field*, then in my work *the field* and its revelations are to be respected above even my own suspicions or possible insights, as was proved by the spontaneous word change in the preceding constellation example.

Investigation

If you are struggling with an addiction to drugs or alcohol, ask yourself, "For whom do I take cocaine?" or "For whom do I smoke marijuana?" Perhaps simply through reading and feeling the preceding case studies you already have an answer. If not, write on a piece of paper a simple family tree, and fill in as much as you know in terms of who's who. Place an asterix next to the name of anyone you know of who died young or tragically. The next step is to simply look at the name and feel in your body if there is a response. This simple but effective exercise may begin to reveal your own inheritance of grief and trauma that has been passed down from generations before you. Understanding this process is a big step towards finding solutions to your own destructive addictions.

Greg
"I can't help myself"

Payne: What would you like to work with today?

Greg: Mostly my drug use. I'm what you might call a party animal. I've been using crystal, cat and various other substances, all together with alcohol, marijuana, poppers, everything. I just can't help myself.

Payne: Are you in a relationship?

Greg: No, I've never really had a stable relationship, just one that lasted a few months here and there. I'm gay and I spend most of my time in the club and party scene.

Payne: So what brought you here today?

Greg: Well, I'm 35 and I've realized that I can't continue to live like this. I have lots of friends, I'm always busy, but there is an emptiness in my life. I've tried to find answers in other areas like meditation and Eastern thought, but none of it to date has answered my emptiness.

Payne: Please tell me about your family of origin.

Greg: I have a brother and a sister, I'm the youngest child. My folks are still married, nothing out of the ordinary, well, except me of course *(laughs)*.

Payne: I enjoy your sense of humour, but it is an interesting comment to make, nonetheless.

Greg: Yeah, I suppose so.

Payne: So tell me about your mother's and father's families.

Greg: Oh, there's quite a lot there, I think.

Payne: Well, just start were it is easier to start.

Greg: Well, my father was one of six, and one of his brothers drowned in a back-yard swimming pool when my father was about nine years old. His mother then went on to drink and became an alcoholic. Then, in

Chapter Five – Addictions and Substance Abuse

my mother's family – let me think – my mother was the fourth child, and then there was a fifth, a girl. She died at birth, and not a stillbirth as far as I know, but she died a few minutes after birth. My mother remembers hearing her mother scream and then her aunt taking her off somewhere else as this was happening. My mum said that she had been forbidden to ever talk about her sister ever again. In fact, her aunt told her that she had never really had a sister as she did not live when she was born, so she was to forget it.

Payne: OK, let us investigate. Select representatives for your father, yourself, your mother, her sister who died at birth, and your father's brother who drowned in the swimming pool.

Greg hesitates a little and after composing himself he selects the representatives and places them according to his feeling.

U: Uncle F: Father M: Mother A: Aunt G: Greg
GF: Grandfather GM: Grandmother

Figure 1

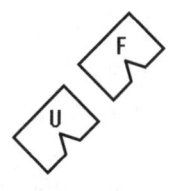

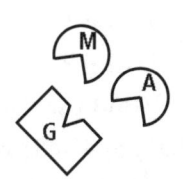

Payne: The first thing I notice with this configuration is that you cannot see your father and that you look hemmed in with your mother and aunt.

Greg: Sometimes I do feel suffocated by my mother.

Payne: Let me investigate.

Payne to Greg's Representative: How are things here?

Greg's Representative: It's intense. I can hardly breathe and I feel fixed to the spot.

Payne to Mother: How are things with you?

Mother: It's a mixture of fear, grief, bewilderment, all sorts of things going on.

Payne to Aunt: And with you?

Aunt: I don't belong here, but I feel stuck here, unable to move.

Payne to Father: How are things with you?

Father: I'm glad that my brother is next to me. I feel a little sad, but my main focus is my son and my wife. It's like I'm not part of them at all.

Payne re-organises the constellation and puts them in a more flowing order.

Figure 2   U F M   A

                G

Payne to Greg's Representative: How are things now?

Greg's Representative: A little better, but I still feel this strong pull towards my mother and my aunt.

Payne to Mother: How are things now?

Mother: I'm very confused. It is difficult with my sister next to me and my son over there. I want them both close, but not as close as before. It's like I can't choose between my sister and my son, so I have to see them together in some way.

Aunt: I'm still not comfortable here, I don't feel free.

Payne: Where would you feel free?

Aunt: Over there. *(Aunt points backwards to her left.)*

Payne: Please move there.

Mother: Oh, no, that's terrible.

Greg's Representative: I feel the urge to move, as well.

Payne: Follow your impulse.

Greg moves and stands next to his mother, in the place where his aunt stood. His mother smiles at him broadly.

Payne to Mother: Whom do you smile at when you look at your son that way? At your son or at your sister?

Mother: *(Crying)* My sister, I still see my sister next to me, even though it is my son.

Greg's Representative: It's true. I don't know who I am here. I feel that my aunt must stand next to me.

Chapter Five – Addictions and Substance Abuse

Payne: OK, let's look at that.

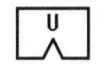

Figure 3   ⊔U ⊔F ⌒M ⊔S ⌒A

Payne: How is that now?

Greg's Representative: Like at the start, I feel suffocated, but I also feel a strong impulse to stand here.

Mother: It's very confusing; I can't tell the difference between the two of them. No, it's more like I can't live without them, her, him, I don't know.

Aunt: I'm in the wrong place again and I feel shackled.

Payne takes representatives for the grandparents (Mother and Aunt's parents) and places them in the constellation. He moves Greg's representative to stand next to his father.

Figure 4

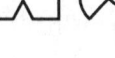

G   GF   GM

F   M   A

U

Payne to Greg's Representative: How is that next to your father?

Greg's Representative: Better, but I'm still drawn there.

Payne: Well, let's see what happens once we've done some work over there.

Payne to Grandmother: How are things here?

Grandmother: Deep, deep grief.

Grandfather: Also sad, but I sense a kind of inner resolve to hold things together.

Payne to Mother: How are you?

Mother: I'm trembling all over. I have a childlike feeling that I will be punished.

Payne to Grandmother: Please move closer to both of your daughters and place one hand on each of their shoulders and look in your living daughter's eyes.

Payne asks Grandfather to stand behind his wife, gently supporting her with a hand on each shoulder.

Payne to Grandmother: Please say to your living daughter, "This is your baby sister, she left us very early, but she is still your sister".

Grandmother: *(Through tears)* This is your baby sister, she left us very early, but she is still your sister.

The representative for Greg's mother bursts into tears and flings her arms around her sister. Both of her parents hold both children.

Payne to Grandmother: Please say to your living daughter, "You have my permission to take her as your sister".

Grandmother: You have my permission to take her as your sister.

Payne to Mother: How does that feel when she says that?

Mother: It's such a relief. I finally have a sister.

Greg the client begins to cry heavily whilst sitting in his chair during this part of the constellation.

Payne to Greg: What's happening?

Greg: When she said that it was such a huge relief, it was like a huge weight lifted off my shoulders.

Payne asks Greg's representative to sit down and places Greg in the same position, next to his father.

Payne to Mother: Please look at your son and say to him, "This is my sister, your aunt, and you are only my son".

Mother to Greg: This is my sister, your aunt, and you are only my son.

Greg sobs once more and his father's representative spontaneously holds his hand.

Payne to Greg: What is happening for you?

Greg: Finally, I can be myself. This is so confusing, but it all feels so true. I'm still not sure if I'm my father's son. I feel like an alien that has just arrived here.

Payne to Greg: Please look at your father. Do you notice how he smiles at you?

Father: It's a relief to have him next to me.

Payne to Father: Say to your son, "The safest place for you is next to me".

Father to Greg: The safest place for you is next to me.

Payne to Greg: Please look at your mother and say to her respectfully, "I'm safer next to Father".

Greg: "Dear Mum, I'm safer next to Dad".

The representative for Greg's mother smiles at him and gently says, "OK", whilst nodding her head slowly.

Payne: We're complete for now. Let's sit down again.

Payne: So how are you doing now, Greg?

Greg: I'm a little shell-shocked, so to speak. But I feel so different, like I have my own life. I knew all of the feelings, they were so very known, I just never imagined the scenario and how intense it could be.

Payne: It is not an easy fate when you represent someone who has died early in the family. As you represented the dead, I can imagine that all the partying and the drug-taking was the only thing that made you feel alive?

Greg: *(Wiping a gentle tear from his eye)* Yes, without it I felt pretty dead, numb inside. The drugs allowed me to have feelings, but I guess they weren't real feelings after all.

Payne: Well, exaggerated ones. Now please be gentle with yourself. This is a journey and the work has just started. You will have to learn what it is to feel without the drugs and the parties, and not all of the feelings will be positive ones, but allow them to be anyway. We'll keep in touch and monitor your progress, OK?

Greg: Yes. Something big has changed for me today, but I also realize that it's the beginning of a journey.

Summary

As Greg's mother was forbidden to acknowledge her sister, it would appear that she transferred all of her feelings to her son. The Soul does not allow us to exclude anyone or anything; therefore, Greg's aunt was included by Greg's taking her place, a very difficult and burdensome fate. When an individual within a family system replaces someone who died so young or tragically, very often they carry the feeling of being dead. In Greg's case, his drug usage and "being a party animal" would appear to be the only way he knew how to be alive.

I have worked with other clients where this dynamic is not only nearly identical, but also they carry the same name of the person who died. When this happens, it is a more clear-cut sign that the family system has sought a replacement.

I have also worked with some individuals who are convinced that they are the reincarnation of the dead child from the previous generation. Whilst I do not dismiss this possibility, my focus is purely on the family system. Reincarnation belongs to another realm of the Soul, one that is beyond the focus of this type of family work. Let us suppose for the moment that Greg was indeed the reincarnation of his mother's sister. What then? The answer is that Greg is Greg today and the solution remains the same. Therefore, I do not find it fruitful to enter into such conjecture.

Chapter Six

WHOSE LIFE IS IT, ANYWAY?

Over the past several years, I have met a number of clients who have left an indelible mark on my own Soul as they have entrusted me with a part of their journey towards healing. Elize is such a woman. Although I am not using her real name, Elize has graciously agreed to allow me to share some of her story with you. When she first contacted me by phone, I found her abrupt, a little demanding, and I decided in advance that she was going to be a "difficult client". At that stage, I had no idea of the gifts that she would bring not only to me, but also to my students and some regular clients who witnessed her gracious transformation.

As her initial telephone contact was simply to book for a workshop, I at that stage knew nothing of her background. On the day she arrived for her first workshop, I saw her walking up my driveway towards the workshop space. She was sporting a leather cap and knee-high leather boots and my first thought was, "She must be Jewish, and her family died in the concentration camps". It was as if I were watching a Gestapo or SS officer walking towards me. Her demeanour, her clothing and her energy all seemed to resonate with perpetrator energy.

As the workshop progressed through the day, her insistent and commanding energy continued and, quite reluctantly, I agreed to work with her, although she was not scheduled to set up her own constellation until the following Sunday. This is what transpired.

Elize
"They all died in Auschwitz"

Payne: What would you like to work with?

Elize: My marriage. My husband won't listen to me. He puts his nose behind a newspaper and it feels as if I am not there.

Payne: Have you been married for long? Do you have children?

Elize: We've been married for more than thirty years and we have two children.

Payne: Have there been any significant events in your marriage, such as miscarriages, stillbirths, major illnesses or the like?

Elize: No, nothing like that, although I was diagnosed with bipolar disorder about six years ago.

Payne: Are you under professional care and are you on medication?

Elize: Yes. I'm on quite high doses of three different kinds of medicines.

Payne: Are you or have you been suicidal?

Elise: No, not really. There have been some periods when I've been in deep depression, but nothing serious, no attempts.

Payne: Please tell me about your family of origin.

Elize: Why do you want to know about them? The problem is with my husband.

Payne: In this work, we find that patterns we inherit from our families and entanglements with the events of the past have a major influence on our current relationships.

Elize: Well, I'm Jewish. I had a twin sister who died a few years ago, but as an adult. Plus I have two other siblings.

Payne: Did anything special happen in your father's family?

Elize: Well, he has one living sister. He came to South Africa when he was very young.

Payne: Did he leave Europe because of the Holocaust?

Elize: Yes, he and his sister were the only survivors out of a family of seven. His parents and other brothers and sisters all died in Auschwitz.

Payne: That's a lot in one family. My preference is that we start with your family of origin, rather than with your husband. Such profound family trauma has a deep residual impact, and taking into consideration that you're bipolar, I feel that it makes more sense that we start with your father's family. Is that OK with you?

Elize: I'm still not sure how this has got anything to do with my husband not talking to me.

Payne: My experience tells me that if we set up a constellation to look at yourself and your husband, the chances are that it will go in the direction of your father and Auschwitz. It is such a major event in your family's history, we can't really avoid it. That is my advice, but it really is up to you.

Chapter Six – Whose Life is it, Anyway?

Elize: I'll go with your experience.

Payne instructs Elize to select representatives for her father, each of his dead brothers and sisters, her grandfather, her grandmother and herself.

GF: Grandfather   GM: Grandmother   S: Sister   B: Brother
F: Father   E: Elize   UR: Unnamed Representative

Figure 1   (S)   [GF]   (GM)   (S)   [B]

                        (E)   [F]

As this constellation was set up, the tension in the room was very palpable. Payne noticed just how emotionally cold Elize appeared to be as she set up the constellation, even to the point of almost "man-handling" the representatives as she placed them. For the most part, clients usually place representatives in a gentle and thoughtful manner, but Elize was almost disdainful.

Payne to Elize: How is it for you when you see them all and your father looking at them?

Elize: I don't know. I'll see what you do.

Payne to Elize's Representative: How are things here?

Elize's Representative: I'm rigid. I feel nothing. A little curious. But otherwise nothing.

Payne to Father: How are things with you?

Father: It's like I'm not even here.

Elize interrupts

Elize: That sounds like my father; he didn't talk to me, either.

Payne: How does it feel when you look at your own representative when she reports feeling nothing and that she feels rigid?

Elize: I don't know *(shrugs shoulders)*.

Payne: Would you like me to continue working?

Elize: Yes.

Payne notices that the representative for Elize's father has started to shake.

The Language of the Soul

Payne to Father: What's happening here?

Father: It feels like I am going in and out of my body. One moment I'm simply not here, not present at all, the next moment I'm shaking. This is too much for me.

Payne talks to the man who is representing Elize's father. His name is Jonathan and he is momentarily out of the role.

Payne to Jonathan: Are you finding the role too much?

Jonathan: Yes. It's very intense. I've had tough roles before, but this is overwhelming.

Payne: Should I choose someone else?

Jonathan: No, I think it will be OK.

Payne: Try to simply report what you are feeling rather than allowing it to take you over so completely. I can take you out and replace you whenever you want. Just let me know.

Jonathan steps back into the role and the constellation continues. The energy in the room is "thick" and a couple of individuals who are observing are looking a little nauseous.

Payne to Father: How are things with you now?

Father: I have a strong feeling to be with them. It is an overwhelming urge.

Payne: Follow your impulse.

The representative for Elize's father crosses the workshop space towards his family and stands with them. He then collapses and the representatives for his family who all perished in Auschwitz hold him. The scene is heart-wrenching, and although I have become very accustomed to seeing such scenes and remaining very neutral, a tear rolls down my cheek at this scene. It was haunting beyond scale and the wails of the father reverberated within the workshop space. As I looked around the room, everyone was either looking deeply moved or was crying. A moment later, another Jewish client of mine spontaneously started reciting the Mourner's Kaddish:

Yeetgadal v' yeetkadash sh'mey rabbah

B'almah dee v'rah kheer'utey

v' yamleekh malkhutei,b'chahyeykhohn, uv' yohmeykhohn,

uv'chahyei d'chohl beyt yisrael,

ba'agalah u'veez'man kareev, v'eemru: Amein.

Chapter Six – Whose Life is it, Anyway?

Amein. Y'hey sh'met rabbah m'varach l'alam u'l'almey almahyah
Y'hey sh'met rabbah m'varach l'alam u'l'almey almahyah.
Yeet'barakh, v' yeesh'tabach, v' yeetpa'ar, v' yeetrohmam, v' yeet'nasei,
v' yeet'hadar, v' yeet'aleh,
v' yeet'halal sh'mey d'kudshah b'reekh hoo. b'reekh hoo
L'eylah meen kohl beerkhatah v'sheeratah,
toosh'b'chatah v'nechematah, da'ameeran b'al'mah, v'eemru: Amein
Amein
Y'hei shlamah rabbah meen sh'mahyah, v'chahyeem
aleynu v'al kohl yisrael, v'eemru: Amein
Oseh shalom beem'roh'mahv, hoo ya'aseh shalom,
aleynu v'al kohl yisrael v'eemru: Amein
Amein.

A great peace descended on the room and all was still again.
Payne to Elize's Representative: How are things now with you?
Elize's Representative: A little moved, but nothing really.
Payne to the Client Elize: And for you?
Elize: I'm not sure I understand the relevance. *(She shrugs her shoulders.)*
Payne takes an unnamed representative and places him the constellation.

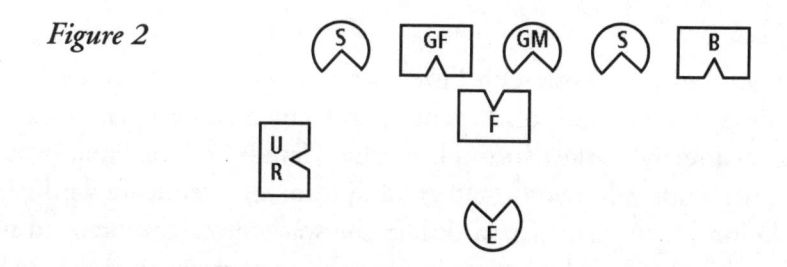

Figure 2

Payne to Elize's Representative: Does anything change when I bring in this representative?
Elize's Representative: Yes, I'm more interested in him.
Payne asks the representative to sit down and works directly with Elize.
Payne to Elize: How are things now that you are standing here looking at your family?

The Language of the Soul

Elize: I'm angry. They were all so weak.

Payne: Yes, I noticed the look of disdain on your face.

Payne: What happens when you look at this representative *(pointing to the unnamed representative standing towards her left)*?

Elize: I'm curious; I'm comfortable with him here. Who is he?

Payne: We'll get to that in a moment. Would you like to stand next to him?

Elize crosses over to stand next to the unnamed representative.

Payne: How does that feel now?

Elize: Much better. I'm comfortable here.

Payne: And when you look at your father and his family?

Elize: I'm still angry with him.

Payne: Look at the man next to you, look him in the eyes and tell me what you feel.

Elize: I feel comfortable here; better than being over there *(pointing to her father's family)*.

Payne: Do you have any idea who this man is?

Elize: No, no clue. But I'm OK with him.

Payne: He's the camp commandant at Auschwitz.

Elize shrugs her shoulders and Payne ends the constellation.

I continued to work with Elize over a period of several months. During that time, she became softer, gentler and much more open to the idea of working directly on the issues of her father's family and the Holocaust. At one stage, her husband, a very gentle and kind man, attended a workshop with her. During that particular workshop she was able to comprehend not only that her bipolar disorder had an impact on her marriage, but also, as her first constellation had shown her, that she was strongly identified with the Nazis and carried perpetrator energy. Today Elize is very fondly regarded by many who are regular attendees at my workshops, as she has blossomed into a gentle woman with quite a sense of humour.

I wanted to share this particular story in this chapter as it serves to illustrate how, when we are identified with the perpetrators of the past, we have no sense of self and it is as if we are leading another person's life, not our own. Another reason to share this story that has been told in brief on these pages, is that I have come to learn that we cannot underestimate the far-reaching impact of trauma, even when that trauma is not related to our own direct experience, but to our parents' or our grandparents' experience. It is generally known that victims of violence or sexual abuse can become perpetrators themselves later on in life, but it is not generally known, that the descendents of victims can also become perpetrators, or carry perpetrator energy that moulds their general disposition.

Elize continues to get in touch with more of her essential self as her entanglements with the past are resolved through Family Constellation work.

Aaron
"My brother died before I was born"

Aaron is a young man in his mid-twenties. He reports feeling a great pressure in his life to perform and to be perfect.

Payne: What would you like to work with?

Aaron: As I mentioned earlier, I feel this great pressure to be perfect all the time and I'm always telling myself that I'm not good enough. When I read your book, some things seemed to fall into place.

Payne: What happened in your family?

Aaron: My eldest brother died before I was born. I didn't really think of him as my brother until I read your book; it struck a chord somewhere.

Payne: How did he die?

Aaron: It was what they call a "cot death". He was just a couple of months old at the time.

Payne: Do you have any other siblings?

Aaron: Yes, a sister.

Payne: Are there any other events in the family that you know of?

Aaron: No, that's really it.

Payne: OK, please choose representatives for yourself, your sister, your father, your mother and your brother. Does he have a name?

Aaron: Ariel.

The Language of the Soul

S: Sister   F: Father   M: Mother   A: Ariel   Aa: Aaron

Figure 1

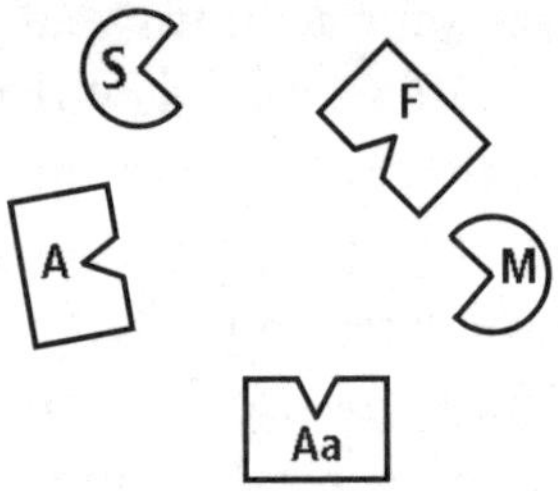

Payne to Mother: I notice how you are looking at your living son, Aaron. What's happening?

Mother: It's nice to see him, although he's not standing that close to me.

Payne to Mother: Are you able to look over there at Ariel?

Mother: No, that is too difficult.

Payne to Aaron's Representative: How are things with you?

Aaron's Representative: I feel like I am outsider looking in. I get a little irritated when my mother looks at me, and I feel no contact with my father.

Payne to Sister: How are things with you?

Sister: I feel quite uncomfortable here, it feels tense.

Payne to Father: How are things with you?

Father: I can't feel anyone else, I feel disconnected, a little numb.

Payne to Ariel: How are things here?

Ariel: I feel cut off; I'm not sure why I'm here. No one is looking at me.

Payne to Aaron's Representative: How do you feel when you look at Ariel?

Aaron Representative: I feel a little aggressive, also sad.

Payne to Aaron the Client: How does this feel for you from there?

Aaron: I feel annoyed, very annoyed. It's like they expect me to be my brother and I have to be extra perfect because of it.

Payne: These feelings have always been there?

Aaron the Client: Yes, but watching this has brought it into focus. My mother only looks at me and not at my father or my brother. That's how it feels.

Payne: Well, we'll work with this and see what happens.

Chapter Six – Whose Life is it, Anyway?

Payne takes Ariel and places him directly in front of both parents.

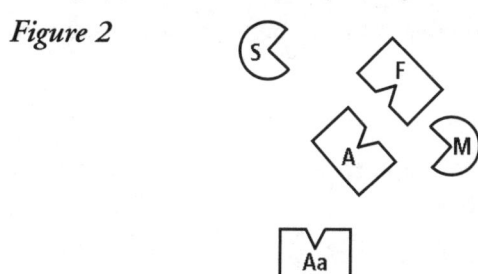

Figure 2

Payne to Father and Mother: Please look directly at your first born child, your son.

Mother begins to shed tears profusely. Payne takes a representative for her own mother, and places her behind her for support. He follows suit with the father and brings in his father.

Payne to Father and Mother: Please embrace your child.

Payne to Sister: How is it for you when you see this?

Sister: It's a relief, and also moving to finally see it.

Payne to Aaron's Representative: And how is it for you now?

Aaron's Representative: Also a relief, but I'm still a little agitated.

Payne to Father: How are things for you now?

Father: I can feel my son now and see the others. It's good to feel my wife, too.

Mother: It feels good to see my husband and to feel my mother and son.

Payne places Ariel with his back up against his parents so that his parents can both feel him and see their other children.

Payne to Parents: Please look at your second son and say to him, "This is your brother, the first born, and you are our third child".

Parents: This is your brother, the first born, and you are our third child.

Payne to Aaron's Representative: How does it feel when they say that to you?

Aaron's Representative: It's a relief. I feel much more relaxed now.

Payne: Please look at your elder brother, Ariel, and say to him, "You are the first, I am only the third".

Aaron's Representative: I don't want to say that, "only the third".

Payne: Well, it's true.

Aaron's Representative: I know, but I still don't want to say it.

Payne: Please try.

Payne turns to Aaron the client.

Payne to Aaron the Client: He seems to have difficulty with saying this. How do you feel?

Aaron laughs a little. Payne replaces Aaron's representative with Aaron the client.

Payne to Aaron: Please look at your elder brother, Ariel, and say to him, "You are the first, I am only the third".

Aaron: *(Smiling broadly)* I can't say it either.

Payne: OK, try this. Say to your brother and parents, "I'm the most important one".

Aaron: I'm the only important one.

Payne: Hhhm, you say that with quite a lot of confidence.

Aaron: Well, no one else is doing anything to solve the problems in the family.

Payne: So that makes you more important?

Payne to Father: Please say to Aaron, "This is your brother, and he is first. You are my third child".

Father: This is your brother, and he is first. You are my third child.

Payne to Aaron: How is that now?

Aaron: That's a little better.

Payne now re-arranges the constellation according to hierarchical order.

Figure 3

Payne to Aaron: How does that feel now?

Aaron: Actually OK. I feel relaxed here. I can see both of my parents and my mother is looking at us equally.

Chapter Six – Whose Life is it, Anyway?

Conclusion

Aaron was clearly in a difficult position. His mother was looking only at him and could not look at her dead son, Ariel. This was felt deeply by Aaron and that would answer his feeling of "having to be perfect" – in a sense, trying to be both Ariel and himself. However, as part of his rebellion against this, he fell into the trap of making himself bigger, which in itself creates problems for him. In doing so, he interferes with the natural hierarchy of the family and further alienates himself from his father. When we approach such constellations, it is not as straightforward as saying that there is only one issue that needs to be resolved. Very often multiple issues come to the surface that are intertwined like mesh. Step by step, Aaron can begin to take his rightful place in the family. At the end of this constellation, I had Aaron say to Ariel, "I take you as my brother". This allowed love to flow between them instead of resentment from Aaron.

When I have worked with individuals who have lost a sibling at an early age, there have been generally two long-term reactions. Either they feel guilty for living and often do not allow themselves to live life fully, or they feel resentment towards either the parents or the dead sibling. This normally stems from the feeling either that they are no longer seen, as the parents only focus on their grief, or that they must strive to excel in everything they do in order to be "perfect children". A step-by-step approach to constellation work can heal these wounds successfully and create order where there was once disorder.

Amanda
"I don't know who I am"

Amanda came to one of my workshops as she had a deep sense of being lost and not knowing her place in the world. During her first interview she shared with me that the firstborn of her family was a little girl who died at the age of two from an illness. Amanda was born just two years later. On further investigation, Amanda reveals that her parents' first child had also been named Amanda. This gave my client a deep sense that she did not exist and that her only task was to be the other Amanda for her parents. She shared that she had tried changing her name through using her middle name at times, but that nothing had changed this feeling that she was simply a replacement and that she had no intrinsic value other than that. Her fate, admittedly, was not an easy one. Her path with constellation work was quite arduous and at times she felt like giving up. Through representatives she began to develop a relationship with her sister and also began to feel the difference between them, and eventually she succeeded in feeling her own identity.

I've worked with several other clients who have experienced similar situations and almost identical feelings. One young man was named after his mother's brother who died at the age of six, and another young man named after his maternal grandfather who died when his mother was a young girl.

In some families, it is traditional that children be named after one of the grandparents. In my experience, when parents name a child after someone who died either tragically or at a very early age, they are transferring their wish for the return of the one they lost onto the child, and this in itself creates a burden. It is as if the mother or father is saying, "You will now represent the one I loved and lost". For the most part, this transference is subconscious and parents do this feeling that it in some way honours the dead or missing person. In reality, however, it creates a burden.

Chapter Seven

ANCESTRAL INHERITANCE

The sins of the fathers will be visited on the children and on the grandchildren to the third and fourth generations.

Exodus, Chapter 34, Hebrew Scriptures

Many of us are very familiar with this biblical quote. Whilst I see no room or evidence for an external force that can "punish" us for the deeds of our forefathers and mothers, what this book and my previous book, *The Healing of Individuals, Families and Nations,* highlight is the principle of "that which is excluded will be included". However, there is a little more to it than that. For example, with the case studies given both in this book and in my previous book, we have clearly seen that when a child dies young, or when another individual dies tragically and their fate is not accepted, this exclusion can lead to another individual, perhaps two or three generations later, representing the deceased individual or event through carrying either their feelings or living their fate. What is also apparent is that the experiences and the resulting emotions, fears and trauma can often span many more generations than two or three. Additionally, we have seen that when perpetrators are viewed as less than human, they too become excluded and are therefore represented in a later generation, furthering the seemingly endless cycle of perpetrators and victims. The descendents of victims themselves can re-enact the actions and feelings of their ancestors' perpetrators.

During a "Movements of the Soul" workshop held in Johannesburg, some of the more seasoned participants in Family Constellation work wanted to connect with their ancestors in order to experience the power of their support. With some of these constellations, much more was revealed than had been expected.

Tania, a woman of Afrikaans descent, explained that her family had been in South Africa since the end of the 17th century and that they were Huguenots, of French Protestant descent. I instructed her to select as many representatives as she felt intuitively appropriate to represent her French ancestors and set up a constellation, placing herself in the constellation so that she could feel their presence. What was immediately apparent was that her Huguenot ancestors all looked sad. What came next was a surprise to her fellow students, not least to Tania herself. Tania proceeded to lie on her back on the floor, holding her stomach, and she cried in a manner that expressed the deepest of grief. She later reported that she had experienced a terrible physical pain in her lower abdomen and that the grief was beyond anything that she had ever experienced. Tania is well known to me and, through observation and by her own admission, she has had a life-long struggle to feel emotion, any emotion at all. However, during her time as a student of Family Constellation work, which was also supplemented with body work, she began to open up slowly and gradually to the world of feelings and emotions. In order to bring about some resolution, we then placed representatives in the constellation to represent those who were missing. After a while, all became calm and Tania reported feeling released.

What we know is that the Huguenots experienced terrible persecution in France. Many Huguenots had their children forcibly removed and "re-educated" in Catholic convents while the parents had to flee France and leave their children behind. Many children were also secreted away in the dead of night and placed on ships to countries where they would be safe – America, England, South Africa and the Netherlands. In earlier waves of persecution against French Protestants (Huguenots), many were burnt at the stake and had their homes razed to the ground. What this illustrates is that large-scale trauma of this nature is passed down through the generations to us today, having a residual impact on our emotional state, fears and even phobias. This has implications not only for descendants of the Huguenots, but also for the descendants of African slaves, Jews and many other persecuted groups.

An important question to ask is, From how far back can the experiences of our ancestors touch us today? In another "Ancestral Workshop", a student wanted to connect with her ancient British ancestors. As the representatives for her ancestors stood there, they reported being "very old", meaning from long ago, not just a century or two. As the student and the ancestors stood there, after about a minute one reported, "There is something here that I don't like", pointing to an empty space beside her. Several others reported feeling it, as well. Knowing that these ancestors were very old, I thought about the history of the British Isles and the various invaders who had come

Chapter Seven – Ancestral Inheritance

their way. With this in mind, I decided to investigate the possibilities of who or what that feeling was and placed, in silence, with no mention of who the new representatives were, various eras of British history and the invaders. In went the Normans of 1066; no response. In went the Vikings; no response. Then to my surprise, in went the Romans and the response was phenomenal and very palpable. None of the representatives knew who this new character was, only that they were not comfortable with its presence.

Payne to Diane: How do you feel when this representative stands here?

Diane: I feel defiant!

Diane reported that her body was rigid and that she wanted to defy this presence with all of her might.

Payne: These are the Romans.

Diane: Well, I don't like them at all!

It was quite amazing to me to see a woman in 2005 respond so strongly to events that had taken place almost 2000 years previously. Who would have thought it? The constellation continued. I placed representatives next to the Romans for all the gifts that the colonisers had given the Britons as part of their legacy: language, religion, and architecture.

Payne to Diane: Look at those next to the Romans and bow to them.

Diane: I refuse! I won't do it.

Payne: These are the gifts that the Romans gave to your ancestors, the gifts that you live with today as their descendant. Do you know what they may be?

Diane: I'm still not bowing to them.

Payne: The gifts are language, religion and architecture. Everything you know as a Western European, and as a Briton, was given to your ancestors by the Romans. They changed and influenced the language of Western Europe, they left their architectural mark and developed technology. Later, the Holy Roman Empire brought us the Christian religion. Almost everything you identify as your culture belongs to the Romans.

Diane tried for several minutes to bow to the Romans, but couldn't.

Payne: Look at your ancestors. To whom are you loyal?

Old Woman: It's me.

Diane: Yes, it's her.

Payne to Old Woman: Please look at your descendant, Diane, and say to her, "This is my war, leave it with me".

Old Woman: This is my war, leave it with me.

Diane: It's still very difficult. I would be disloyal to her and everything she did if I bow to them.

Payne to Old Woman: How does this feel when you see her being so defiant?

Old Woman: In a way I am proud, but it is of no benefit to her.

Payne to Old Woman: Say to Diane, "You dishonour me by fighting my battles for me", and tell me how it feels when you say that.

Old Woman: You dishonour me by fighting my battles for me.

Old Woman: It's right. I'm quite capable of fighting my own battles.

Diane lets out a sigh of relief.

Diane: I'm ready to bow now. *(Diane bows gracefully.)*

Payne to Diane: How does that feel now?

Diane: I'm a little stunned by my strength of feeling. My entire life I have rebelled against authority, even breaking some minor traffic laws out of defiance. I never suspected this. I feel relaxed now, it's like my defiance has melted.

Diane reported in the weeks that followed that she no longer defiantly broke minor traffic laws and that her feeling of "me against the world" had disappeared. She, and not least myself, could not have even imagined that such patterns of behaviour could have come from so far back in history. It gave all of us much food for thought. A few months later, Diane attended a Family Constellations Christmas party for the students, who were invited to come dressed as their favourite ancestor. As may be predictable, she came dressed as an ancient Briton, battle axe in hand, with helmet and shield. Another student of Italian descent came, equally predictably, dressed as a Roman, replete with toga and a leafy garland in her hair. It was amusing to observe the friendly banter between them that expressed echoes of those ancient loyalties.

History teaches us that each war begets the next war, even generations later. This is the power of our loyalty to ancestors. How then do we create a world of peace when at times we are faced with inner impulses that instinctively make us either trust or distrust certain nations, groups or

Chapter Seven – Ancestral Inheritance

ethnicities? Family Constellation work, which has as its foundation psychotherapeutic process, can assist us in healing relationships. It also has a much broader application where we can give our ancestors a voice and begin to disentangle ourselves from hidden loyalties that do not serve us as individuals, nor as groups or nations. We can no longer see ourselves as individuals separated from those around us nor, as it would appear, as being independent of our ancestors. In many cultures it is believed that the ancestors are always with us, and this would appear to be more true than perhaps any of us have ever imagined. Healing the past is the key to healing the present and indeed the future. How, then, do the sons of plantation owners in the Americas look at the sons of African slaves and feel peace in their hearts? How do the daughters of Huguenots look upon the daughters of Catholics with deep acceptance? Peace begins in the Soul. An inner movement to embrace, accept and submit to the fate of our forefathers and foremothers is a movement of the Soul. The Soul includes all experiences and all people without exception. All events are part of a rich tapestry of experiences that have contributed to the evolution of humanity. Just as one war begets another, war also begets peace and ushers in periods of technological and social change. War has been in our yesterdays, is with us today, and will be in our tomorrows until we as a species embrace our evolutionary journey with the grace and humility it deserves. The invading forces that subjugated my ancestors have created the very language in which I write to you in this moment, English. Am I to despise the English language? Or am I to embrace it as a gift woven out of the cloth of war?

I am reminded of a science fiction television series I saw, in which a man who had lost his beloved wife devised a "time ship" in which he could erase events of the past in order to create a history in which his wife had not been killed. As the fabric of time unravelled entire civilisations, worlds and species were eradicated forever, as if they had never existed. The results were catastrophic for his present time. This episode served to remind me that when we ignore, deny or resist fate and what is, the consequences are far-reaching and the cycle of suffering simply continues unabated.

Ancient battles

Probably the oldest battle of them all is the one that is still being fought between Jews and Christians and the Islamic peoples of the world. It would seem that the distrust between Christians and Muslims is as alive today as it was during the Moorish invasions of Spain, the Crusades and the expanding Ottoman Empire.

As the above story of Diane and her Romans expresses, hidden loyalties can survive not only for several generations, but also for millennia. When we look at biblical history, we perhaps have other answers to explain the enmity between the Judeo-Christian world and Islam. Isaac was not Abraham's firstborn, or only, son. Fourteen years before, when Abraham was 86 (Genesis 16:16), Sarah (then called Sarai) had arranged for a child to be born to Abraham through her own Egyptian maidservant, Hagar. Ishmael was born from the arrangement (Genesis 16:1–4). Traditionally, the Jews are the descendents of Isaac and his son Jacob, whilst the Arabs are descendents of Ishmael. Ishmael was the firstborn of Abraham, and yet the "Covenant" and inheritance went to Isaac. In addition, in Genesis we are told that, "When she (Hagar) realized that she had conceived, her mistress (Sarah) was lowered in her esteem". Hence, we have an historical record of what could have been the foundation of the tensions between Arabs and Jews. Add to that the Crusades and French and British colonisation of the Middle East, plus today's wars motivated more by oil than by the rhetoric of freedom and democracy, and it is little wonder that we still have strife. As Judaism is the root of Christianity, it then follows that Christian loyalties lie squarely in the Jewish camp.

For many, Islam has the face of dogmatic oppression of women, brutality, and is a religion that lacks compassion, caring and love. However, how far back in our own history do we need to look in order to find the same oppression and cruelty? Not far! As Family Constellation work has shown, our distrust of Islam may stem from the anger we feel at how our own mothers, grandmothers and great-grandmothers were treated in generations gone by. The Islamic world may simply serve to hold up a mirror which in turn will motivate us to heal our own families and nations.

Chapter Eight
MAKING CLEAR APOLOGIES

It would seem that most of us are not particularly good at apologising to those we have either wronged or disrespected in some way. When it comes to apologising, much of what we say in the process comes from our fear of being rejected, and therefore of losing love, or from our reluctance to take full responsibility for our actions. However, this reluctance to take full responsibility for our words and deeds is still rooted in the fear that love will be withdrawn. Much of our resistance to taking responsibility for what is ours stems from not truly understanding the difference between taking the blame for something and taking responsibility. There is a big difference between the two. Deeply rooted in our psyche are the millennia-old belief systems that have taught us that to be blamed means certain punishment or a fall from grace in the eyes of God. For many of us, to err or sin means certain death without redemption. Even though for the most part many of us no longer hold these punitive religious beliefs, they still form the foundation of much Western and Eastern thinking.

The strong sense of shame that has been instilled by the world's dominant religions has spilled over into the general populace and is destined to be carried forward for many generations as we unravel the code of shame that has been passed down from one generation to the next. This code of shame has impacted human behaviour in ways that are immeasurable but are often clearly visible in terms of results, actions and attitude. We only have to look back a generation to see how young, unwed pregnant women were secreted away in order to hide their shame and to avoid disgrace being placed on the entire family. In avoidance of such shame, much bigger causes for shame were created in the process – a denied child, a burden of guilt carried by all. So how do we climb out of the depths of inherited human shame? We do so by learning and practicing the *language of the Soul*.

When distilled truth is spoken, the body relaxes and there is a perceptible out-breath that ushers in the relaxation that follows. When we practice the *language of the Soul* in our daily lives, soon the fear of rejection or condemnation for our transgressions begins to fade and we feel the benefits of living truthfully. What must be stressed here is that expressing one's *opinion* and speaking one's *truth* are two different things altogether. Let me give you examples:

A: I thought it was really disrespectful of you not to pay me back the money you owed me right away, and then avoid my calls and ignore my emails. You have walked all over our friendship and I am very disappointed in you. I am shocked to find out that you are so untrustworthy.

B: I feel disrespected and that our friendship has been undervalued by the outstanding debt.

When we look at example A, we see clearly that creating stories and expressing opinions go hand-in-hand with accusation and judgment, which will almost always place the other person on the defensive. Feel the difference between the two examples given above and sense the response that your body has, sense what happens with your breathing. The real difference between the two examples is that the first expression is punitive in nature; we are seeking to punish the other, making them the bad ones and ourselves the good ones. This never works in practice and it is only through a sense of equality that resolution can be found.

In example B, we own our own feelings and state the problem clearly. Additionally, we are saying that our feelings are only associated with the subject at hand – an unpaid debt. What we need to understand is that one disrespectful action does not define the entire person. When we walk head-on into a situation armed with our stories, opinions and judgments, our punitive tone creates the impression that we are telling the other person that they are a "bad person". Resolution has never been created in this way. So let us now look at the subject at hand: how to make clear apologies.

Apologies

When I was teaching students on a year-long Family Constellations Facilitation Training program, some of the students were having difficulty in grasping the nature of the *healing sentences* that we use during the course of a constellation. In trying to find ways that would better enable them to get a feeling sense of the *language of the Soul*, we set up role-play situations where they could practice giving and receiving apologies. This is how it went:

Chapter Eight – Making Clear Apologies

G is representing a woman whose sister, T, had slept with her husband. In the role play, which taps into an archetype present in the "field", the feelings are real.

T says to G: I'm very sorry. I didn't mean to. He has always flirted with me and, after I split up with my boyfriend, I was feeling a little lonely and so it happened. I'm really sorry and I hope you can forgive me.

Payne to G: How does that feel?

G: I'm furious! The more she spoke, the worse it got.

Payne to T: And how was that for you?

T: Not good. I feel agitated, ashamed, defensive….much worse than before I spoke.

Payne to T: OK, let's now try it using distilled truth and the *language of the Soul,* shall we? Say to your sister the following: "I am deeply sorry, I've wronged you. I no longer have the right to call myself your sister".

T: I am deeply sorry, I've wronged you. I no longer have the right to call myself your sister.

Payne to G: How does that feel?

G: It's a relief. Also, when she said that she no longer had the right to call herself my sister I realized how much was at stake and I softened considerably. I feel totally different than in the first exercise.

Payne to T: And how does it feel for you now?

T: I also feel relieved. I feel the severity of what I've done, but I'm owning it totally now. It actually feels good to look at my sister.

On speaking the *language of the Soul,* both sisters felt relief. The importance of what was really at stake, their sisterhood, came to the fore. When this happened, they were able to look at each other as equals, just as sisters. When equality is born out of such use of language, forgiveness itself becomes a moot point, for when there is equality, forgiveness happens all on its own, no effort involved. One of the challenges to thinking and communicating in this new way is our need to punish. In some way, we feel that meting out punishment to another will somehow vindicate us and bring relief at the same time. It never does. Why then did T, using the *language of the Soul,* say, "I no longer have the right to call myself your sister"? When T spoke these words, two things happened. Not only did she acknowledge the severity of her transgression; she also, in effect, offered up her due punishment. So why didn't G then step in and accept her punishment as recompense for T's transgression? When the *language of the Soul* is *spoken*, it is also heard by the *ears* of the Soul. When we *hear* the crystal clear *language of the Soul*, more often than not, our story dissolves and we get a clear picture of what has really happened and of the possible consequences. When T offered herself up for punishment, G was able to see that she would be losing her beloved sister and that if she agreed to it, she too would suffer the consequences; she would no longer have a sister. That price was too high to pay.

When we have wronged someone

Each of us at some stage in our lives has wronged someone, either out of reaction to friction that already existed between ourselves and the other or simply through carelessness in a less conscious way. How do we deal with that and make it right once more?

Owing to deeply embedded fears of being cast out or abandoned, a fear we developed in early childhood, it is very difficult for most of us to truly own up to and take responsibility for our wrong-doing. Instead, we often find ourselves creating stories that justify in large or small ways the wrong we have done another. Often, the biggest trap is insisting that the other also apologise for their part. But of what benefit is that? Why do we often take this stance? More often than not, we become so invested in the opinions of others that we become frozen in our own lives, unable to move forward. Again, it is our deep-seated fear of being the "bad one" that prompts us to remain stuck when it comes to our own transgressions. As we have noticed through using the *language of the Soul*, the guilty also gain much benefit from expressing distilled truth; the body relaxes and this is coupled with an outward sigh of relief as the truth is spoken, even when that truth highlights our own guilt in the matter. Why is that? The nature of the Soul is to include all that which has been excluded, even when that which has been excluded and denied makes us look guilty. When the *language of the Soul* is heard by the ears of the Soul, it penetrates the heart, and the need for punishment, revenge or recompense most often dissolves. However, what if, after our best efforts, the other person does not respond in a way in which the matter can be simply resolved and resolution can be found? Does it even matter? The short answer is no, it does not make any difference. What is important is that we own with

Chapter Eight – Making Clear Apologies

unambiguous honesty and integrity that for which we are responsible, irrespective of provocation or circumstances that might justify our words or actions. When we have wronged someone, we have simply wronged them; it doesn't get more complex than that. So why do we create so much story and justification behind the instances when we have erred? We often feel that the more we say and the more we explain, the greater the likelihood of our being forgiven by the other. In reality, the opposite is true. Generally, the more we say, the worse it gets, and the less chance we have of the other accepting our apology as offered. We tell our stories because we feel guilty and surreptitiously hope that the more good reason we give, the less guilty and therefore "bad" we will look. It is the fear of being "bad" that is the culprit in all fumbled apologies. It goes back to age-old programming that stems from religious teachings and childhood experience – the good are rewarded, the bad are punished and cast out. Being cast out is the worst thing that can befall any member of a tribe, modern and technological or not. So what if we are "bad"? The absolute truth is that one hurtful action does not define you as a person; it simply defines a moment in time, that is all. If others choose to define you as a person based on that moment in time, that is truly their business and not yours. The judgments we hold about wrongdoing in others are the same judgments we hold about ourselves.

Let me give you an example from a workshop.

Alice
"I have a difficult relationship with my daughter"

Payne to Alice: What would you like to work with?

Alice: I have quite a difficult relationship with my daughter. She is experimenting with drugs and is very rebellious. I am worried for her and the tension at home is becoming unbearable.

Payne to Alice: Tell me about her father.

Alice: He died a couple of years ago.

Payne: Were you still married to him at the time?

Alice: No, we divorced a few years ago when my daughter was ten.

Payne: How did he die?

Alice: He had cancer and he was ill for a long while.

Payne: What was your relationship like with him after the divorce?

Alice: We never spoke.

Payne: How old was your daughter when her father died?

Alice: 17. That was two years ago.

Payne: Did you go with her to her father's funeral?

Alice: No. After we divorced I wanted nothing to with him.

Payne: But your 17-year-old daughter needed you; her father had died.

Alice: I didn't see it like that at the time; I wanted nothing to do with him.

Payne: So it seems your daughter has paid the price for your feelings.

Payne selects representatives from the workshop group to represent Jamie, Alice's daughter, and Jamie's father, Alice's ex-husband. He instructs the representative for Jamie's father to lie flat on his back on the floor, as if in the grave. Jamie's representative kneels beside him and begins sobbing uncontrollably.

Payne to Alice: How is it for you when you look at your daughter?

Alice: It is very painful.

Payne: Who do you think she needs to be beside her in this moment?

Alice: *(Sobbing)* Her mother.

Payne: Yes, her mother. Please go over to her and kneel beside her.

Alice walks over to Jamie's representative and kneels beside her.

Payne to Alice: How is this for you?

Alice: Very difficult, I feel very guilty.

Payne: Guilt only exists when we can't carry our own wrongdoing. Please look into your daughter's eyes and say the following, "Beloved daughter, I have wronged you greatly. My place is beside you".

Alice looks down at the ground, barely able to say the words through tears of grief and a feeling of shame.

Payne: Try to say the words again.

Alice to Jamie: Beloved daughter, I have wronged you greatly. My place is beside you.

Payne to Alice: How does that feel now?

Alice: It's a relief. I felt helpless before; now I know that I can change something.

Payne to Jamie's Representative: How does it feel for you?

Chapter Eight – Making Clear Apologies

Jamie's Representative: I'm still very heart-sore, but it was also a relief when my mother said that to me. My anger with her is subsiding.

The constellation ends and Alice returns to the chair next to Payne.

Payne: The fact of the matter is, your daughter was far too young to attend her father's funeral alone.

Alice: She was also with him when he died.

Payne: And you weren't with her then, either?

Alice: No.

Payne: You need to let go of the fear that these errors in judgment make you either a bad person or a bad mother. It is one period in time only.

Alice: It was a relief to say those words and I see it more clearly now. Until this point I could not even see why my daughter is angry with me. It feels good to have this in the open.

Payne: So has admitting your wrongdoing made you feel stronger or weaker? Smaller or bigger?

Alice: At first, very small, I was afraid of being judged, but as I let the words sink in and sensed that I was not being accused of anything, I felt stronger when the full realization of my wrongdoing came to me. It's a relief.

Payne: So now you can go home and love your daughter. But there is more work to be done here. Whenever you disrespect the other parent, the child is shamed in the process. We'll do some more work in the future with this. Do you agree?

Alice: Yes, anything to help my daughter.

Payne: And to help you, of course. It is difficult to live with such feelings.

Conclusion

Very often when a process similar to this one is observed in a workshop setting, some individuals respond with statements like, "Aren't we supposed to dissolve guilt or rid ourselves of it?" More often than not, in our attempt to dissipate guilt, we create a story around why we did or said what we did. We add in the details of the circumstances of our lives and try to find a justification for our transgression, some of which may be very valid. In doing this, however, we are rarely in a position to truly own what is ours, and therefore the guilt never goes away, but simply lingers on in the background.

The Language of the Soul

After guiding numerous people through this and similar processes, it is clear to me that when we take full responsibility for our words, actions and deeds, instead of being weakened, we in fact are greatly strengthened by full ownership of what is ours. The Soul thrives on truth. When truth is spoken, relief is evident and it usually manifests with an out-breath. As we speak the truth, without masks or pretences, we are strengthened by our Soul's presence. Truth has a universal resonance with that which is higher than ourselves. In those moments of speaking truth, it is as if we become a channel for the greater good, even if it means confessing clearly our own wrongdoing. Masks and the stories we tell to protect ourselves create a smokescreen through which it is very difficult for the light of greater good to shine. In fact, the very thing we are trying to avoid, being seen as a "bad person", is what ends up happening when we create such smokescreens; our light and our Soul cannot be seen at all, for it is far too foggy.

There is great dignity in holding and carrying what belongs to us. When we don't, the vast majority of us find ways in which to sabotage or punish ourselves, in small ways or in larger ways. When we feel the dignity of carrying that which belongs to us, we are supported by our Soul and life gets better and better as we grow from strength to strength. Owning our guilt is not a form of self-punishment; it is a movement towards clarity and truth – the realm of the Soul.

EPILOGUE

Over the past couple of decades, with the rise of self-help books and the growing acceptance of therapy in its many forms as the norm, we have been encouraged to express and speak our truth. However, how do we know when we are speaking our truth or expressing the truth with any level of authenticity? Many of us still seem to waiver between keeping things to ourselves, having learnt that it is not polite to express our true feelings and so we simply sweep things under the carpet, or we blurt out our "truth" with great regularity and offer our opinions and advice whether or not they have been requested. Through the pages of this book we have learnt that truth is simplicity itself. It has no masks, no pretences; it simply is. The key to truth is keeping it simple. No story, no justification, just the facts. But how do we know what a fact is? So many of us assume that our opinions and perceptions are facts when they are only that, an opinion or a perception, nothing more. Until we actually get inside someone else and feel what they feel, our opinion of them is only that, and what we assume to be fact cannot be proven.

Perhaps you will never attend a Family Constellations workshop and your understanding of this work will be more cognitive than experiential. However, even without a workshop, the power of the *language of the Soul* can be experiential for you within hours or days of putting this book back up on the shelf or passing it onto a friend. We have learnt and have witnessed that the *language of the Soul*, also know as healing sentences, is distilled truth and, just like anything that is distilled, it is strong and powerful, something that gets noticed and felt. As we keep our words simple, we clear our mind; as we clear our mind, our greater self, rather than our smaller self that just loves all the stories and the drama, can come forth. Our greater self is our Soul; hence, as we speak distilled truth and feel the peace of that, our Soul has an opportunity to be present in our words, and indeed present within our entire being and experience. Language is such a wonderful gift! Words have meaning; words can change not only one life, but also nations. In years gone by, regimes have forbidden books, they have controlled the use of typewriters, and some countries today even seek to control the flow of information across the Internet. Such is the power of words. Words shape history, religions, politics – and they can heal a lonesome or broken heart. We cannot underestimate the power of words: they can both heal and hurt; they create freedom or repression. Words, whether written or spoken, can shape the destinies of millions or of just one person.

And what of truth? Why is truth so challenging for most of us, not least truth with ourselves? At the beginning of this book I presented much on the subject of sexual abuse and offered a truth that is controversial for many – the truth that the victims of sexual abuse more often than not are bonded to their abuser and usually feel a deep sense of love for them. However, this is a truth that many find difficult; the strong moral imperative that to love one's abuser is simply 'wrong' causes many people to prefer to believe in the lie and pursue punishment over healing at any cost. Some truths are difficult to bear – for example, the gifts of fate. If we are descended from African slaves, for example, the many gifts that come with being an African-American result from that very difficult fate. The *language of the Soul* does not look at what is right or wrong, what is just or reprehensible; it looks at facts — not in a cold way, but in the presence of truth. When we touch the presence of truth, we touch something magical; it is grace, it is the presence of the Divine.

For some, Family Constellation work is yet another psychotherapeutic process that can help us solve some problems we have in our lives. When we experience the essence of the *language of the Soul*, however, it becomes a deeply spiritual experience and, beyond that, a part of spiritual practice.

In the pages of this book, we have ventured into the territory of "representation" as opposed to role play, and we encounter *the knowing field*, or simply *the field*. Now that I have been involved in engagements with *the field* for more than eight years through Family Constellation work, I can look back at my relationship with the intelligence of the field. In my first two years I tried very hard to try and "figure it out". Eventually, I simply gave up and submitted to the mystery of it. What I can tell you is that *the field* talks to me and it knows me intimately. Many a time I have been faced with an issue that has come up I my life and miraculously, as if by design, half a dozen clients with the same or a similar issue come marching through my door and ask me to help them with it. Sometimes it is a little annoying, I will admit to that – none of us particularly likes having our nose rubbed into something – but I have learnt that the intelligence of *the field* is my friend and I have come to trust it. I would like to say that I trust it implicitly; however, like most of us, I keep my intellect in the sidelines just in case I don't "get" what the field is telling me, or one of my own blind spots stands squarely in my way for a while.

We have seen that individuals take on, as if by magic, the feelings, even the physical symptoms, of those they represent. There is no hypnotic suggestion, no group trance state, nothing of the sort. Together with my students, we have tested, re-tested and tested all over again the power and presence of *the field*. Individuals have been placed into constellations with no knowledge of whom they represent, yet they become very clear about who they are. One evening I placed someone in the centre of the room to represent Nelson Mandela. Nothing was said, and not even the person representing Mr. Mandela was aware of their role. The reverence in the room for our "representative" was immediately palpable, and some people felt moved to bow their head to this unknown person. As this was with South African students of Family Constellations, their response was to be expected if they knew who it was, but they didn't. *The field* simply communicated the statesmanlike and Soul quality of the man we have all come to love, respect and admire. So what is really happening? Are the representatives "channeling" the Souls of others? Or are the attendees and students all psychically gifted? In my experience, the vast majority of attendees at Family Constellations are normal people with normal jobs and normal lives who would never consider themselves to be either psychic or empathic. Channeling? Some have wondered, even feared, whether the Soul of another would enter them whilst in a role. However, representatives are equally aware of themselves as they are of the feelings and impressions they gain from a role. So how does it really work? The truthful answer is, I don't really know. Lynn McTaggart's book, *The Field*, gave me some insights into this phenomenon, and that is a very good place to start if you simply "have to know". However, for the most part, it remains a mystery to me, and one that I submit to.

What our adventures and discoveries within *the field* have told us is that we are all connected and belong to something that is far greater than ourselves. Is that God? Is that Jung's collective subconscious? Perhaps neither of these concepts serves *the field* or describes it satisfactorily. What I do know is that individuals who have been represented and were not even physically present in a workshop have experienced spontaneous healings of life-long emotional issues or disruptive life patterns.

When we enter *the field*, we enter the dominion of the Soul. This dominion has no judgment, it embraces both victims and perpetrators, it holds both the innocent and the guilty, it includes everything and excludes no one, it seeks to unite. Perhaps, after all, the field is God, and the field is where we as God's children all play and learn the simple truths of love in its many forms. Make up your own mind. It is powerful, it is present, it is everywhere. It guides us, it holds us, it lifts us, it heals us, it teaches us, it connects us, it binds us together, and it reveals who we are, where we belong, and what are our illusions are. For some, this is the God of Love, for others a mystical healing force, and for still others it is both a mystery and a fascination. What I do know for certain is that *the field* is our friend.

                                        May "the Field" be with you.
                                        John Payne

FURTHER INFORMATION AND CONTACTS

Contact the Author

You may email the author at info@johnlpayne.com or visit his website at www.familyconstellations.net

International and US Workshops

John L Payne accepts invitations to facilitate workshops and training worldwide. He has facilitated workshops in the USA, Netherlands, Norway, Caribbean, South Africa, India, Brazil and Germany.

Invitations to facilitate workshops in any part of the world for groups of 18 or more gladly received.

USA and Canada: Please visit www.johnlpayne.com

South Africa: For workshops in Johannesburg and Cape Town, South Africa, please call The South African Institute for Family Constellations on 011 614 0821. Invitations to facilitate in other parts of South Africa gladly received for groups of 12 or more.

Or email familyconstellations@telkomsa.net

Website: www.familyconstellations.org

Copies of *The Healing of Individuals, Families and Nations* may be purchased via his website or by visiting www.findhornpress.com

Recommended Resources

Carol Kulig: Energy Healer
New York, USA
Website: www.paragenesis.com   Tel: 212 662 7998

Annebiene Pilon: Family Constellations Facilitator
Leusden, The Netherlands   Tel: 033 465 6727

Schools

The Snow Lion Centre International School
Healing through the Human Energy Field
Switzerland
Website: www.snowlionschool.ch

The Barbara Brennan School of Healing
Healing through the Human Energy Field
Florida, USA
Website: www.barbarabrennan.com

The Clairvision School
Healing through Self Investigation and Entity Removal
Sydney, Australia
Website: www.clairvision.org

To obtain a copy of the current Findhorn Press
catalogue please contact us by email:
info@findhornpress.com
or phone: +44 (0)1309 690582.

Alternatively, please visit our website:
www.findhornpress.com